What others are saying about this book:

"This book is a resource for any parent, teacher, or mental health professional seeking real solutions to the difficulties of working with children and teens. In keeping with Dr. Sutton's tradition of offering quality resources, If My Kid's So Nice ... Why's He Driving ME Crazy? exceeds my expectations as a clinician."
—**Richard K. Nongard**, Executive Director, PeachTree Professional Education, Inc., Tulsa, Oklahoma

"I'm so thrilled that Dr. Sutton has taken the time to write this book! He provides a wealth of understanding and practical approaches for dealing with these greatly misunderstood (and difficult) children."
—Mother of a seven-year-old son with ODD, Allen, Texas (name withheld for child's sake)

"I used the concept of the overlapping circles with one mother. She is now listening more and judging less, and is being more introspective. Her daughter is finding her way back to school and is completing homework more readily. Without question, this book shows extensive experience and hard work along with a lot of dedication to working with frustrated parents and frustrating kids."
—**Dr. Miquela Rivera**, clinical psychologist, Albuquerque, New Mexico

"A masterful balance between the professional and practical, ... captivating, usable, understandable examples and ideas for the frustrated parent and teacher."
—**Dr. Darwin F. Gale**, Professor and former Chair, Department of Educational Psychology, Brigham Young University

"Practical ideas that really work. I began to offer my students choices, giving them some control of their day, and saw a drastic reduction in bad behaviors. My two most defiant students became cooperative, pleasant, and present!"
—**Pat Zimmerman**, fifth-grade teacher, Grantsville, Kansas

"Dr. Sutton understands the need for cooperation and compliance in school settings. His book helps school personnel achieve that by giving them strategies to interact with challenging students in a rational, calm, and effective manner. His emphasis on building positive relationships with oppositional and defiant students is fundamental to helping them attain school success."
　　　—Jane Bieri, SED Teacher (Emotional Disorders), Minot, North Dakota

"This book touches a great need for parent education in clinical work with oppositional and defiant children, and is written in a comprehensive, but practical and easy to understand, style. Like Dr. Sutton's training, I found the book helpful, enjoyable, and enlightening."
　　　—Sandy R. Johnson, Director of Professional Development, The Mental Health Center of North Central Alabama, Inc.

"Dr. Sutton's simple yet descriptive models, such as 'The Feelings Model' and the 'Progression of Deviancy' continuum of behavior, are extremely helpful in my assessments and interventions with school-age children and their parents. His distinctions between the characteristics of the 'Good Kid' Disorder and those of Conduct Disorder are equally invaluable in my diagnostic role as a school psychologist."
　　　—Dr. Robert F. Smith, school psychologist, El Paso, Texas

"My wife attended your Oppositional and Defiant Child workshop at the University of Nebraska. Our fourteen-year-old daughter exhibits the classic symptoms. My wife now feels better about things than she has for almost a year. We are already trying to put into practice some (no, many) of your suggestions. Thanks again for your words of encouragement and understanding."
　　　—A relieved father in Omaha, Nebraska (name withheld for the daughter's sake)

If My Kid's So Nice...
Why's He Driving ME Crazy?

Straight Talk about the "Good Kid" Disorder

James D. Sutton, Ed.D.

Friendly Oaks Publications
Pleasanton, Texas

If My Kid's So Nice …
Why's He Driving ME Crazy?

Straight Talk about the "Good Kid" Disorder

by James D. Sutton, Ed.D.

Published by:
Friendly Oaks Publications
PO Box 662
Pleasanton, TX 78064-0662 USA
(830) 569-3586

Reprinted in paperback edition in 2003

Publisher's Cataloging-in-Publication Data

Sutton, James D.
    If my kid's so nice—why's he driving me crazy? / James D. Sutton
        p.   cm.
    Includes bibliographical references and index.
    ISBN 1-878878-65-4
    1. Problem children—Psychology. 2. Oppositional defiant disorder in children. 3. Child rearing. 4. Parent and child. I. Title.

$18.95 soft cover (paperback)

Dedicated in loving memory
to my mother,

Margaret Sutton

and my grandmother,

Myrtle Smith

"And now, my daughter, do not fear.
I will do for you whatever you ask,
for all my people in the city know
that you are a woman of excellence."
—Ruth 3:11 (*NAS*)

Preliminary Statement

From a clinical standpoint, the condition known as Oppositional Defiant Disorder (APA, 1994) has historically been the subject of considerable discussion and even disagreement. Much of what is found between the covers of this book is based upon research gleaned from respected journal articles in the fields of psychology, psychiatry, and education. Much of it is also based upon the experiences of the author, who wrote his doctoral dissertation on the subject (Sutton, 1981). In particular, the models and perspectives utilized were developed by the author over a period of about twenty years, and they have been validated by his use with clients and those participants who have attended his training seminar entitled *The Oppositional and Defiant Child* (Sutton, 1995).

It should be noted that the term "Good Kid" Disorder is not a part of any formal diagnostic system. The term was created by the author to suggest the severity of behaviors of oppositionality and defiance in those youngsters who are not antisocial or without meaningful family connections, and who will likely never be in significant trouble with the law. They are good kids with irritating behaviors.

This book was never intended to be a substitute for competent counseling, therapy, or other medical, psychiatric, or psychological treatment. With this in mind, the author and Friendly Oaks Publications shall have neither liability nor responsibility to any person or entity with respect to any loss or damage caused, or alleged to be caused, directly or indirectly, by the information contained in this book. Any reader who wishes not to be bound by this entire Preliminary Statement may return this book to the publisher for a full and complete refund.

Table of Contents

List of Figures

Acknowledgements

Someone once said of ambitious thoughts, "Take a couple of aspirin and go to bed until the thoughts go away." I wonder if the person who said that ever had thoughts of writing a book. Seriously, I would like to acknowledge four individuals who played a part in making this book a possibility.

First of all, to Bobbie, my wife and best friend for twenty-six years, I owe so much. From running the office so that I could work on a tough chapter, to ongoing support, to cheerfully tolerating having too little of her husband around for much too long, it seems that she is as much the author of this book as I am.

To Virginia Iorio, I am appreciative of the diligence and dedication she gave to the task of editing this book. Her contributions added immensely to the clarity and readability of the finished work.

To Robert Howard, the dust jacket artist, I am in awe, not only for his talent, but for his ability to take the seed of an idea and turn it into something that surpassed my wildest expectation.

And finally, to Zig Ziglar, I express my thanks for his willingness to take the time from his packed schedule to write the foreword. Zig once said that if he had never sold even one copy of his best-seller *See You at the Top*, it would have been worth all the work and effort because of what he gained in writing it. Only now I think I understand what he meant.

Foreword

The title of this book, *If My Kid's So Nice ... Why's He Driving ME Crazy?*, expresses the feelings and sentiments of millions of parents in America. Many parents have good kids, but are frustrated by their behavior. Fortunately, when we begin to really understand what Dr. Sutton calls the "Good Kid" Disorder, solutions become apparent. Hope is rekindled, and our optimism and attitude toward our kids begin to change.

Most of us are periodically discouraged with our progress, particularly in our relationships with our children, especially if we don't have a clue as to what we can do to solve the problem. When Dr. Sutton talks about the "No-lutions," things we do over and over again that simply don't work, it's as if he has spent a few days with all our families. Indeed, he clearly identifies the problems, then goes on to offer logical, commonsense solutions that put relationships back on track.

In many cases, the first thing that will happen is an attitude change on the part of the parents. When they realize that the problem is not really earth-shattering or impossible to turn around, their attitude toward their child changes; insight gives birth to hope. Dr. Sutton offers encouragement and specific suggestions to initiate these changes.

I believe a major reason why *If My Kid's So Nice ... Why's He Driving ME Crazy?* is so effective is because Dr. Sutton asks penetrating questions that require answers. Whenever parents or teachers exercise the insight to see that they are part of the problem, they become empowered to also be part of the solution.

This one concept is so simple, yet so profound. Luke's parents dared to be vulnerable (Chapter Seven), temporarily putting aside their own feelings and frustration in order to find out what was bothering Luke and why he was doing so poorly in school. As a result, everyone got what they wanted and needed, and, with Luke, change came literally overnight. Encouraging.

In most cases, good kids and good parents are not only willing, but anxious, to solve the issues that trouble their relationships. No one really wants conflict as a daily way of life. Dr. Sutton provides the three keys that can unlock the strife: fairness, reasonableness, and a willingness to have a little fun occasionally (can't we all think of families that haven't had *any* fun in years?).

Dr. Sutton's greatest contribution in this book is his ability to communicate to parents the importance of not trying to *change* these children, but rather of empowering youngsters to make the changes *themselves*. Any parent would be well advised to invest time in studying this book and following the suggestions for intervention. I also encourage parents to make an additional investment and give their child's teacher a copy of this book. That way, teacher, parent, and student will all be "on the same page." Good stuff.

Zig Ziglar
Dallas, Texas

Editor's note: Zig is a world-class speaker, best-selling author, and Chairman of the Board of the Zig Ziglar Corporation. His books include *Raising Positive Kids in a Negative World* and *See You at the Top*. His most recent book, published by Thomas Nelson Publishers, is entitled *Over the Top*.

Preface

The log of calls coming into my office over the past year or so has somewhat resembled a national registry. The most recent were from Sacramento, California; Lexington, Massachusetts; and Minot, North Dakota. These calls had a couple of things in common: the Internet, and an interest in more information about working with the oppositional and defiant child.

Most of these calls were from parents. Almost desperate for information on managing a son or daughter diagnosed with Oppositional Defiant Disorder (ODD), they were looking for some help. This book is a response to that need.

Two things should be in place before this book will deliver the help that was intended. First of all, parents or teachers who attempt to employ the interventions discussed in this book must make the interventions their *second* priority. Their first priority should be an attempt to understand the youngster *behind* the oppositional and defiant behavior. It is only through understanding and insight that the interventions stimulate maximum change.

Secondly, manifestations of oppositional and defiant behavior constitute a wide range of deviancy. This book was not intended to cover the entire range, but rather the youngster with the "Good Kid" Disorder. This youngster understands family and social connections, and is very rarely in trouble with the law. With this youngster, concerns cluster around problems of compliance and resulting consequences, poor progress or failure in school, and strife within the family. It's been said that this child is in trouble not so much for what he or she is *doing*, as for what he or she is *not* doing. It is important to add, however, that youngsters can vary a great deal in their dispositions and behaviors.

Additional resources and support are recommended for the youngster whose behaviors exceed those covered in this book, or for parents who have difficulty implementing the suggestions and interventions. In these cases, a highly structured parent training program, such as the one developed by Dr. Russell Barkley of the University of Massachusetts Medical Center, is recommended (Barkley, 1987).

Because it is difficult to realize instant "cures" with oppositional and defiant children (although Chapter Seven will address how some youngsters and their families *can* realize permanent change quickly), some of the actual cases mentioned in this book are still ongoing. Different names were used for these youngsters in order to protect them. Rest assured, however, that the youngsters and their stories are very real indeed.

It is my desire that you find this book not only helpful, but heartful and hopeful.

JDS

Chapter One

Pager Panic

Beep-beep! Beep-beep! Beep-beep!

Whoever invented the pocket pager should be forever haunted by his own creation. I pulled it from my waistband and checked the number. Unfortunately, I recognized it, but somehow managed not to chuck the thing into the San Antonio River.

I looked around for a phone. Only one mystery remained. Was it Doug's mother or the boy's father who was trying to reach me? If any kid had ever developed a skill for driving his parents to the telephone in wild-eyed hysteria, this twelve-year-old had it down cold.

Actually, Doug could have taught it. Professor of Parental Insanity has a nice ring to it.

I found a pay phone. While dialing the number, I braced myself for either of two emergencies. If it was Dad who had put out the page, he would be angry, annoyed that all of this "psychology stuff" wasn't working with his kid. He would inform me that Doug had brought home yet another failing slip from school, and that he was just about ready to apply his own brand of remedy to the boy's backside.

On the other hand, it could be Mom. She would call to say that things between Doug and Dad were worse than ever, adding that if it weren't for her being there to referee, there could be *real* trouble between these two. Then, on a long exasperated exhale, she would add something about not knowing how much more of this she could stand.

The call was from Doug's father. I could not have been more accurate in my prediction of what he would say, except that Doug had collected *two* failing notices—and Dad had already applied his remedy.

Something Powerful

If the relationship between Doug and his family sounds painfully familiar, there's a good reason why. You are not alone in the predicament. Unfortunately, there are times when it is not much comfort to know that other parents are also struggling with their kids; you just want the trouble to stop.

Doug, Mom, and Dad were caught up in something powerful, something that seemed intent on hurting all three of them. As a child and adolescent psychologist, one of my primary aims in helping a family like this one is to be of meaningful service without becoming the *next* victim. Oppositional and defiant behavior in children and adolescents can be that potent and destructive.

The oppositional and defiant child is the subject of breakfast table conversation on any given morning in countless homes across this country; kids like Doug fill a diagnostic category (Oppositional Defiant Disorder) to overflowing. It's a serious concern made even more serious by the fact that traditional interventions work poorly, if at all. In family counseling centers across this country, parents are telling us that oppositionality and defiance are among the most irritating behaviors they observe in their children. It is no coincidence, then, that these behaviors are the very ones that parents do not manage well at all. They are searching for some answers. Left to their own ways of handling things, Mom, Dad, and their oppositional and defiant child tend to move in the same direction—the wrong one.

An Obvious Fact

The heat of battle with their seventh grader had seemingly blinded Doug's folks to a rather obvious fact: he had a great deal of control over them. What's more, he loved it. Doug had come upon a way to work his father into a full lather and turn his mother into one big walking ulcer. The lad had arrived at a most effective way of keeping up an intense relationship with his folks, albeit a painful one. As a bonus, he had his teachers wondering if any student could possibly be more irresponsible.

Doug had accomplished all of this in a very unique and creative manner. He did it simply by doing nothing.

Linda

Linda was living proof that oppositional and defiant behavior isn't something reserved for boys. She was a bright, but bitter, third grader who had her stepmother ready to check into the nearest hospital.

Following the divorce of her parents, Linda moved in with her father. Things went fairly well until Dad remarried; then it all fell to pieces. The house was a war zone for Linda and her stepmother. The situation got considerably worse when Linda took a pair of scissors and cut all the bristles off of her stepmother's favorite hairbrush.

"I didn't know it was *yours*!" Linda later exclaimed, punctuating her concern with tears.

Linda was failing the third grade. The reason: no homework was being turned in. The stepmother could not understand this, as she made certain that Linda completed her schoolwork every evening. Why, she even made Linda show it to her before she went to bed.

Sometime later, the stepmother solved the puzzle. She found all of the missing homework hidden away in Linda's dresser.

Kevin

I encountered Kevin as a referral early on in my career as an assessment specialist for a school district in southern Texas. The teacher's remarks on the referral would become very familiar ones to me:

"Sometimes silently ignores directives."

"Tends not to do things when told."

"Does not do what is required in the classroom."

These remarks could have been rubber-stamped into the assessment folders of the hundreds of Kevins (*and* Dougs and Lindas) that I eventually encountered.

This fourth grader was failing miserably. His folks were upset beyond description. The problem with Kevin was certainly not a lack of brains or potential. In fact, he was two grade levels ahead of his class in most areas of achievement.

This boy's father was a white-collar professional. His demands upon his son mirrored his very loud and blustery, hard-drinking nature. Mom, a more passive soul, was uncomfortably sandwiched squarely between the two.

Kevin was scared out of his mind—terrified, really. But he didn't know it, at least not consciously. Kevin spoke of a fear of storms, earthquakes, and tornados, and of being torn to bits by them. Within the safety of these symbols, young Kevin was probably describing the anger and rage of his father. He was in great fear of the man, and his building resentment was being played out against Dad in the only way that seemed to be reasonably safe and effective.

I can't remember things changing much in Kevin's case. My lack of experience certainly had something to do with it.

A Good Kid

What impressed me about Kevin was the fact that, aside from the irritation and grief he was causing his teacher and parents, he was basically a good kid. He had plenty of friends, didn't roam the streets at night, and seemed to have regard for the law and the rights of others. Aside from the fact that he was unusually quiet and reserved (observations I would later learn to investigate as possible symptoms of low-grade depression), he was more than appropriate during my work with him. His behaviors of non-compliance at school, however, put him on the brink of failing the fourth grade, and nothing I could suggest to his teacher or parents seemed to make much difference at all. I was stumped, but challenged.

My Search

I tried to read up on kids like Kevin, and again ended up stumped and challenged. The term Oppositional Defiant Disorder was not to come into play for ten or more years, and professional literature on oppositional or passive-aggressive behavior was sparse at best. Fortunately, during this time I came upon two great teachers, Dr. Nick Long in 1976 and Dr. Bob Algozzine in 1981 (see References). I had only a few hours with each of them, but their contributions to my understanding were priceless. Although they didn't realize it, their insights encouraged me through my doctorate and dissertation on youngsters like Kevin.

Front Porch Reunion

As chance would arrange it, I ran into Kevin fourteen years after I had first worked with him as a fourth grader. We shared an exchange of introductions, actually reintroductions, on his front porch. I had been in the process of calling on folks in the community as part of a church canvass of our community.

I tried not to stare at him, but something strong was tugging at my memory. Then I realized that this was the *same* Kevin I had worked with when he was nine years old.

I suppose that the clincher to this front porch reunion would have been either that Kevin had shed all of his problems and was doing quite well, or that he had made finalist for Jerk of the Year. But neither of these extremes seemed to apply there on the front porch that Saturday morning. Like most everyone else, Kevin fell somewhere in between.

What really concerned me the most, however, was the deep sense of sadness that seemed to have settled in behind Kevin's wide, exaggerated smile. Through the years to follow, I became quite familiar with that expression.

The visit troubled me—deeply. I was struck with the realization that my best opportunity to help Kevin had come and gone. I left his house feeling something that I can only describe as a sense of painful, unnecessary loss. This book grew out of that experience.

If My Kid's So Nice ... Why's He Driving ME Crazy?

Chapter Two

Anatomy of Conflict

Just how do frustration and anger develop in the first place? Anger can be expressed in many different ways, some direct and some indirect, but what really brings on the sort of conflict that gives rise to oppositional and defiant behavior?

To arrive at an answer to this question, a behavior that is distinctly human must be considered. It is the ability to set and work toward goals.

Goals and Needs

Individuals who feel that they are sufficiently self-directed also have a basic idea or plan about the direction of their lives. Although few folks ever become involved in the active process of developing concretely expressed written goals, most usually do have some sort of a general plan in place. As long as this plan remains in clear focus, individuals can mentally and physically invest themselves in future events. Only one thing will seriously disturb goal-directed activity—a deep-seated problem with one's needs.

Needs can be as basic as food, air, and water. They demand to be met in much the same way that a newborn demands to be changed, fed, or held. Needs must be met before any energy can be directed at setting or achieving goals. Indeed, if an individual is having difficulty with essential needs, goal-setting will be a meaningless and frustrating activity.

Consider this example. A child comes from a very impoverished and difficult environment, a place where life itself is a day-to-day struggle for survival. In school the teacher asks her to draw a picture about what she wants to be when she grows up. The child might find this task uncomfortable, for the bulk of her energy is directed more toward securing a cracker than a career. Hope and survival are not directly connected to goals; they are first connected to needs.

The oppositional and defiant youngster is not starving for something to eat, but he or she is running short in the needs department. There are seven of these basic needs (see Figure 2-1):

Need #1: Security. This need addresses the essentials, such as food, shelter, clothing, and personal safety. These are a must for survival; everything else is built around them.

Need #2: Order. This need addresses things like predictability of circumstances and elements within one's life. This is exactly why people like to have a schedule, and it is why children and adults alike feel uncomfortable when things in their lives are changed. Even small changes, like a modified schedule at school for a day, cause some youngsters to experience considerable distress. Order, in providing predictability, also provides a sense of safety and control.

Security
Order
Belonging
Worth
Approval
Stimulation
Growth

Figure 2-1

Need #3: Belonging. This need concerns an individual's innate desire to affiliate with others. Churches exist not only for worship, but for fellowship. The child who tells you that he doesn't care if anyone likes him, or if he ever has any friends at all, is either lying or has a serious problem.

Need #4: Worth. Self-esteem (the recognition of self-value) and the ability to self-actualize are central within this need. It is a need around which many of the others are constructed.

Need #5: Approval. This need relates to the desire for affirmation from others. At a very basic level, approval and affirmation are verification of not only an individual's effort, but his or her existence as well. Oppositional and defiant youngsters especially have difficulty with this particular need.

Need #6: Stimulation. Human beings were not engineered to just sit around, vegetating and collecting cobwebs. They require activity, a mission, to function at peak efficiency. If you don't believe in having some activity available for a child, just try sitting with a three-year-old through a one-hour church service.

Need #7: Growth. This need points to more than mere existence. It affirms that every individual can improve in some way every single day. Even though everyone eventually has to deal philosophically with the issue that the body declines, that decline does not have to signal the end of growth. For certain, personal growth is more than physical attributes or abilities; it's a life-long process. Who among us could not become a better husband, wife, parent, or grandparent, or learn to appreciate others more, or exercise more patience and understanding? As a wise person once said, "When you're green, you're growin'; when you're ripe, you rot." What wisdom—age has so little to do with growth.

Life's Messengers

Whenever one or more needs are not being met, serious concerns emerge within individuals regarding the purpose, direction, and even the continuation of their life. For this reason, all human beings have a built-in alarm system, a system that alerts them to problems within the state of their needs. This system is an individual's feelings.

Feelings are the messengers of needs. Folks who are content, basically happy, and of good disposition know it. They are alright in their needs. It's not even necessary that all their needs be met perfectly, but it is important that individuals be able to receive and interpret for themselves the information that their feelings bring to them. The four most critical feelings are *Sad, Mad, Glad*, and *Scared*.

Three of these feelings, *Sad, Mad*, and *Scared*, help to signal concerns in those needs that require some sort of attention or repair. One feeling, *Glad*, indicates the absence of problems. It is the essence of serenity, balance, and stability.

This little model is simple; that's the beauty of it. These four feelings are so basic that a three-year-old can understand them quickly, and even provide a face to go with each one of them. I have seen plenty of forty-three, fifty-three, and sixty-three-year-olds, however, who had the dickens of a time interpreting and utilizing the messages provided by these four simple feelings. Without accurate information from these messages, these individuals can be locked out of the ability to *understand* their needs, let alone deal with them. Their feelings shut down and are of no real use, except to make things worse. It's a miserable way to live.

A Central Feeling

Consider the Feelings Model in Figure 2-2 for a moment. In suggesting that growth moves toward happiness and serenity (*Glad*), emotions of sadness and depression are at the center of everything. Essentially everything passes through *Sad* before it reaches the top. I don't believe that it is any coincidence that, during times of greatest loss and grief, a person experiences the comfort and reassurance of friends and family. In other words, *Sad* brings with it corporate support and hope.

Feelings of *Scared* and *Mad* are valid and necessary emotions, but they do not in themselves contribute to growth. They were intended to be temporary, to signal a problem in the state of our needs, then to be reinterpreted through *Sad* as some form of loss (if only the loss of the feeling of *not* being angry or afraid). Since it hurts so much to be sad or depressed, if even for a short time, some folks prefer to postpone the experience indefinitely, or even permanently. In doing so, they stay fearful and angry (*Scared* and *Mad*). Have you ever known someone who was shut down to living on just these two emotions?

I'm convinced that addictions to drugs, alcohol, and rage often begin as attempts to bury painful feelings (*Sad*). When feelings are buried, needs worsen because the messengers are not being heeded. These needs then fester and become sick. Conflict with others develops, as well as intense conflict with self.

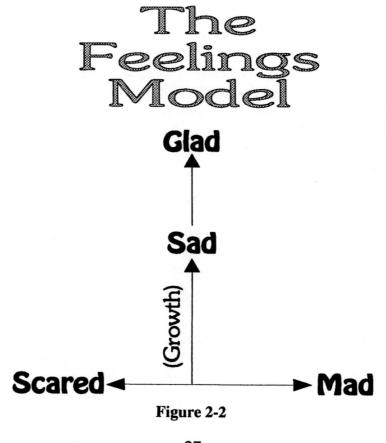

Figure 2-2

One form of conflict in good and decent kids is oppositional and defiant behavior. It might sound workable enough in theory to explain to these youngsters that they have to go through a little pain (*Sad*) in order to resolve the conflict, but these children are fearful of the vulnerability they would have to expose in the process. They need help. This is what the following chapters are all about.

Stewart

At the very time that I was putting this chapter together, I met a courageous nine-year-old boy. I'll call him Stewart, although that is not his real name (none of the names mentioned in this book are real names). His mother had died of cancer and the only other significant adult female in his life, his grandmother, was in a nursing home recovering from some serious health problems of her own. Stewart's father ditched him, then left the country. A relative obtained power of attorney from the grandmother, booted Stewart's older sister from the house, and dropped Stewart and another sister off at a children's home. He then sold the house out from under the grandmother.

The folks at the children's home were concerned that Stewart was challenging them and struggling with them at every turn. They wanted to know why he was being so defiant.

Can you believe it? Mental health professionals make a *lot* of money figuring out the answers to questions like these! Frankly, I would have been seriously worried about

Stewart if he *hadn't* exhibited some rather reactive behavior.

The door to Stewart's feelings had slammed shut, excluding all but two, and at this point you know what they were. That's right—*Scared* and *Mad*. He was being bombarded with messages, messages telling him that he was in deep trouble in *all* of his needs. Not only were key figures in his life no longer available to him, he was not able to receive the soothing and nurturance they had given him in the past. He was left to grieve major losses completely on his own, with only a nine-year-old's insight to comfort him. This kid had started off The Game of Life with five cards in his hand, and ended up with only one. As far as Stewart's outlook on things was concerned, the world was not only cold and indifferent toward him, it was downright vicious and anxious to put him away for good.

Why wouldn't such a child be oppositional and defiant, if not worse? Stewart had a death grip on that last card. No one was going to take it from him. No one.

If My Kid's So Nice ... Why's He Driving ME Crazy?

Chapter Three

To Care,
But to Control

Caring

Fortunately, the uncomfortable dynamics of the relationship between oppositional and defiant youngsters and their families involve little apathy. Although this may not always appear obvious, it is absolutely true. Caring does not come with a switch conveniently marked "On" or "Off."

Caring may often be disguised or sometimes flatly denied altogether during conflicts and struggles, but in the end, it's there. This is good, because hurt inflicted with indifference heals poorly.

I had one young patient once who well illustrated this underpinning of caring. The school suggested that the boy be placed in a GT (Gifted and Talented) program. As soon as he was put into these classes, he began failing *everything* at school. Things weren't much better at home. When the parents brought the boy to my office for an evaluation, I privately asked the youngster what I could do for him. "Tell my folks that I *really do* love them. I don't mean to hurt them," he shared with tears filling his eyes. I took him to be genuine and sincere in what he shared, but even so, the problem behaviors continued.

I believe that it is this bond of caring, then, that operates to simultaneously build and tear at the relationship between frustrated parents and defiant children. On the one hand, caring serves to limit extreme behaviors. Think about it. You don't generally hear of the oppositional and defiant child running with gangs, assaulting folks on the street, and stealing vehicles. On the other hand, caring can indirectly serve to prolong absolutely irritating behaviors such as forgetting, irresponsibility, absolute disorganization, and creatively disguised (and sometimes not-so-disguised) expressions of anger.

Control

Such caring, a reflection of emotional investment, is so intense that it will not budge. A sort of game develops. The playing surface is life itself, with the point and purpose of the game being that of control. This game, when left to run free, never really ends. It simply continues on and on, but at a price.

There it is—a need to care, but a need also to control. Regardless of what the problems look like on the surface, caring and control lie at the heart, the tender core, of the conflict that both binds and burdens relationships.

These two, a need to care and a need to control, pull powerfully in opposite directions. When energy is focused on one, the other festers. More than equal to the struggle, the Dougs, Lindas, and Kevins of the world can give their parents, teachers, counselors, and other child service professionals absolute fits.

A Tough Challenge

As an ex-public school teacher, and now a practicing psychologist specializing in the training of professionals who diagnose, treat, teach, counsel, and manage school-aged youngsters, I see this one, the oppositional and defiant child, as the toughest of all challenges. In fact, many child service professionals would say that this youngster is even tougher to work with than the one who is making splinters of the furniture.

In a four-year study, researchers Cantwell and Baker (1989) found that youngsters who were formally diagnosed with Oppositional Defiant Disorder (a diagnosis applied to oppositional and defiant behaviors when they become persistent and serious) had the poorest recovery rate of all the behavioral psychiatric disorders of children.

I agree with these findings; their results fit with what I have seen in my own research and practice. Obviously, the oppositional and defiant child and his or her behaviors should be taken seriously.

Typical Behaviors

Here's a rather obvious, but profound, statement:

The oppositional and defiant youngster is identified through his or her behaviors.

With this child, behavior communicates as powerfully as if the youngster were calling us on the telephone. These oppositional and defiant behaviors cluster into three groups: Psychological Distress, Inefficiency, and Manifestations of Anger. Figure 3-1 summarizes the fifteen oppositional and defiant behaviors. Although it is likely that you will identify many of these behaviors in your child, it is not necessary or likely that you will observe them all. Let's discuss each in turn:

Psychological Distress. These are emotional states that are usually signaled by behavior.

1. Low frustration tolerance. Because this child is already frustrated, tolerance for any additional frustration is very low. For this reason, this youngster is apt to react negatively to stresses that appear to be minor concerns to others.

2. Irritability. Closely associated with low frustration tolerance, irritability is the "Don't mess with me!" posture that communicates volumes. I often describe irritability as nitro and glycerine snuggling up together for a long ride down a bumpy road.

Oppositional & Defiant Behaviors

Psychological Distress
Low frustration tolerance
Irritability
Synthetic affect
Fear & anger
Depression

Inefficiency
Forgetting
Poor concentration & organization
Procrastination
Strong potential/poor output

Manifestations of Anger
Pouting & stubbornness
Noncompliance
Obstructionism
Blaming & spitefulness
Argumentativeness
Provocative behavior

Figure 3-1

3. Synthetic affect. Affect describes a person's observable presence of feelings (or the lack of them when they *should* be there) as they are seen by others—sort of an "outside" picture of inner emotions. For example, a person who just locked their keys in the car would present an affect of worry and frustration. In the case of the oppositional and defiant child, affect usually consists of some sort of a smile. Such a smile is said to be synthetic because it doesn't "fit" with what the youngster is usually experiencing on the "inside," such as sadness, frustration, anger, and fear. With the oppositional and defiant child, the "outside" and "inside" affects do not match. Mental health professionals refer to this mismatch as incongruency; the child is often completely unaware of it.

4. Fear and anger. Although these are present, the youngster will often try to either make light of them (minimization) or deny them altogether. Sometimes fear and anger are minimized or denied without the full conscious knowledge and understanding of the youngster. This is called repression, a form of automatic emotional self-protection. Repression explains why traditional counseling approaches with this youngster are often less than effective. How can a counselor help a child who isn't even aware of having a problem?

5. Depression. To the best of my knowledge and memory, I have found depression to be a component in every oppositional and defiant youngster I have ever assessed or counseled (with the exception of some of those youngsters who later developed into the disorder known as Conduct Disorder). Much like fear and anger, depression can be minimized, denied, or repressed. Psychologists use tests and techniques called projectives to assess the presence and degree of emotions like depression, fear, and anger.

Inefficiency. These behaviors are neither accidental nor occasional. They are intended to extract their pound of flesh from you-know-who. The fact that unaddressed behaviors of inefficiency persist from year to year indicates that they are unbelievably successful. Again, the full impact of the intent of these behaviors might not always be within the child's complete knowledge or understanding.

6. Forgetting. Here's a form of subtle retaliation that can never be proven. Clever, huh? It represents a handy and safe tool for creating wholesale aggravation. There is no limit to what can be forgotten. Homework, permission slips, jackets, lunches, P.E. clothes, overdue library books, report cards, and important appointments are all prime examples of the forgetter's craft.

7. Poor concentration and organization. The presence of previously mentioned sadness, fear, and anger can boil and bubble, affecting a youngster's ability to focus on tasks at hand. Consequently, the work is apt to be done poorly, if it is done at all. Organizational skills are also affected, a reason why this youngster's room or school locker and desk all look like disaster fallout areas.

8. Procrastination. Although putting things off is a behavior common to all of us from time to time, the oppositional and defiant youngster has raised it to an art form.

9. Strong potential/poor output. The prime topic here is school achievement. The ability is there, as reflected by achievement test scores, but performance in school is heavily pulled down by incomplete or missing assignments. As a thirteen-year-old once said to me, "I could make straight 'A's' if it wasn't for homework!"

Manifestations of Anger. The following represent the degree of direct behavior that this youngster is apt to show us. In terms of their directness, these behaviors are much bolder and "in-your-face" than those of inefficiency.

10. Pouting and stubbornness. This is foot-dragging behavior that causes adults to go ballistic. We tell the child to hurry, then we observe as they actually slow down, or worse yet, grind to a complete stop.

11. Noncompliance. Usually this behavior is initiated in silence without excuses. The youngster, however, has made an outright decision *not* to comply, whether it be with schoolwork or chores at home. For this reason, noncompliance is generally considered to be one of the most directly confrontive behaviors that this youngster displays.

12. Obstructionism. This behavior directly blocks or impedes the progress and activity of others. If the family is planning to go out to dinner with friends at 6:30 p.m., this kid doesn't even show up at the house until almost 7:00 p.m. At school, this student can frustrate other youngsters by getting between them and whatever it is that they want to accomplish.

13. Blaming and spitefulness. This behavior is also pretty direct, intended to pass responsibility off on someone else or seek a bit of restitution for perceived injustices.

14. Argumentativeness. With this behavior the youngster attempts to catch the adult making a mistake, then challenges the adult on it. Often the gesture is disguised as "I was just trying to be helpful." Sometimes, however, the gesture is not disguised at all.

15. Provocative behavior. The ability to create chaos and evoke the ire of others by doing little or nothing, or by being extremely annoying, is the specialty of the oppositional and defiant child. Provocative behavior is typically directed at the values and priorities of the parents and teachers, which is certain to arouse them *and* move them to action. Thus, failure in school could be viewed as a provocative act, especially if Mom and Dad are strong believers in the value and importance of education.

What's Normal, Anyway?

To a degree, oppositional and defiant behavior is normal, a component of appropriate development in children and adolescents (Wenning et al., 1993). Such behavior is especially observed in the developmental stage affectionately referred to as "The Terrible Twos," then again during puberty and early adolescence (the very reason why every junior high school teacher should be eligible for sainthood). During both of these stages youngsters learn to be resistant as they actively oppose authority in attempts to assert themselves as individuals. If not allowed a bit of "growing room," youngsters could develop long-term difficulty with skills of appropriate assertiveness and general coping ability.

Rey (1993) suggested that oppositional and defiant behaviors cease being normal whenever "their magnitude, inflexibility or persistence at later developmental periods would justify their being considered deviant." He went on to add that the formal diagnosis of Oppositional Defiant Disorder "should be made only in the presence of distress or disability." Of course, assessing the "presence of distress or disability" is highly dependent upon those who have to tolerate it.

As a rule, twice as many boys as girls are diagnosed with Oppositional Defiant Disorder among children ages twelve and younger (Anderson et al., 1987; Cohen et al., 1987). In adolescence, the girls seem to take the lead (Kashani et al., 1987; McGee et al., 1990).

What Do You Call It?

For the remainder of this book, the term Oppositional Defiant Disorder (capital letters) will be used as it applies to a formal diagnosis included in the *Diagnostic and Statistical Manual of Mental Disorders IV* (APA, 1994), usually referred to as the *DSM-IV*. The words "oppositional and defiant" (lowercase letters) or "oppositionality and defiance" will be used to refer to behaviors, whether they have ever been formally diagnosed or not (or are even serious and persistent enough to warrant a diagnosis). But diagnosed or not, the behaviors associated with psychological distress, inefficiency, and manifestations of anger are identical.

The subject of the next chapter is the range of behaviors (called a behavioral continuum), from acceptable to severely disordered, and just how oppositional and defiant behavior fits into it.

Chapter Four

The "Good Kid" Disorder

To parents with an oppositional and defiant child living under their roof, the words "Good Kid" Disorder probably sound like an oxymoron. Just about any parent of an oppositional and defiant youngster can think of a number of words to describe their kid—and *good* isn't one of them. Even so, this is an excellent way to describe the youngster who is rarely in trouble for what he *is* doing, but rather for what he is *not* doing (although we will also be looking at some oppositional and defiant behavior as a precursor to a more serious disorder). As one parent put it, "My child doesn't act *out*; he just doesn't act *right*." There is tremendous wisdom and insight in those words.

All behavior that could be considered "good" or "bad" exists on a continuum, a range from one extreme to the other. In terms of behavior, a child who forgets to turn in his math homework would be considered more "good" than a child who is turned in for car theft. But is the child who forgets to turn in his math homework for six or seven years still more "good" than a youngster who steals a car only once? It's an interesting question.

Figure 4-1 is an example of a continuum of behavior. "Good" behavior is on the far left, represented by the white box directly below the words "Progression of Deviancy," while "bad" behavior is on the right (represented by the black box). The behavior of every child and adolescent, every single one of them, falls somewhere on this line. A child who is at point 5 or 6 in the Progression of Deviancy is considered more "bad" or deviant than a child whose behavior is at point 2.

The shaded areas in the figure (not counting the part that is completely black) range from about point 1.5 to point 6 in the Progression of Deviancy. These areas represent the presence of some or all of the fifteen symptoms or manifestations of oppositionality and defiance that were discussed in the last chapter. You will notice that some of these behaviors can even be found in the area called Acceptable Behavior, meaning that they are just a part of normal development, or that they occur only occasionally.

As negative behaviors progress in deviancy (move toward the right), not only is there an increase in oppositionality and defiance, deviancy itself becomes a more persistent part of a youngster's total personality. There is increased resistance to change as a child takes on the features of Oppositional Defiant Disorder. Fortunately, most oppositional and defiant youngsters never progress beyond point 5; this will be discussed more in this chapter.

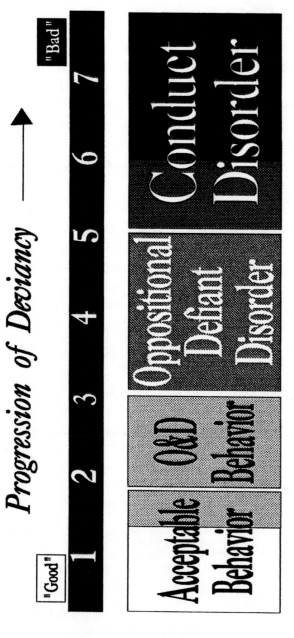

Shaded areas represent presence of oppositional and defiant "symptoms." As noted, they range from acceptable behavior to features present in two major childhood psychiatric disorders.

Figure 4-1

There are those youngsters whose persistent oppositional and defiant behaviors begin to merge with law-breaking behavior somewhere between points 5 and 7. Psychologists and psychiatrists would then apply the diagnosis "Conduct Disorder" to this youngster; it's the most serious *DSM-IV* behavioral classification for a child or adolescent (APA, 1994). At age eighteen, the youngster with Conduct Disorder assumes the adult diagnosis of Antisocial Personality Disorder.

Interestingly enough, the *DSM-IV* contains *no* adult classification for Oppositional Defiant Disorder. Reason: oppositional and defiant behaviors are included in a *number* of psychiatric diagnoses of adults. Obviously, oppositional and defiant behaviors of adults can create great difficulty in relationships. The addressing of these issues could be another book in itself.

But take heart. If you are reading this book as a parent of an oppositional and defiant youngster, the chances are excellent that your child is *not* at points 5, 6, or 7. This is because the desires and hopes of caring parents, especially those parents who actively make change happen, rarely fall outside of the awareness of their children. These youngsters generally respond to these changes, with some degree of *immediate* improvement being noted.

The "Comeback Point"

You won't find the term "Good Kid" Disorder in any other literature. I made it up—which means it's not really an official "disorder" at all, but it is a handy term for some behaviors that are a concern for many parents. It aptly describes the youngster who has the ability to show marked improvement in behavior (meaning *less* oppositionality and defiance). That improvement can result not only from his or her desire to change, but also from all the resources, conditions, direction, and encouragement available to make that change happen. In short, this child can "come back" to acceptable behavior.

Roughly speaking, the youngster with the "Good Kid" Disorder can range anywhere from point 2 to almost point 5 on the Progression of Deviancy scale. Regardless of where a youngster's behavior falls between those measures, however, several characteristics usually apply. With the consideration that there are always exceptions, the following list describes the essence of the "good kid" in the "Good Kid" Disorder:

Characteristic #1: This youngster has social skills. This child typically comes from a family that places a high value on social skills, and attempts to model them. The youngster understands the tremendous power of appropriate social behavior. Consequently, this child is aware of social innuendo and how to use it. This social innuendo might include telephone etiquette ("She's not in right now, but I'd be happy to take a message"), social interaction ("Thank you very much for inviting me; I had a wonderful time"), what to say to someone who has lost a loved one ("I was sorry to hear that you lost your grandfather"), and seasonal greetings ("Have a very Merry Christmas and a Happy New Year").

Characteristic #2: The child understands love and affirmation. This youngster knows that there are folks who, beneath their frustration, deeply care about him or her.

Characteristic #3: Academic ability is not the problem. Although this youngster might not be performing well academically in school, ability is not the issue. The typical oppositional and defiant child is capable of performing at age and grade level, or better.

Characteristic #4: Many of the youngster's behaviors are indirect. Behaviors such as forgetting, procrastination, obstructionism, and underachievement are "disguised" carefully so that they do not appear to be direct. Although argumentative at times, this youngster is usually aware that there is a limit to it, and does not become violent, even verbally. It is unlikely that this child would ever be involved with the police.

Characteristic #5: This child craves more autonomy. Although not lacking power and influence (as in the power to make *your* stomach knot and churn), these youngsters feel that autonomous choices are limited or nonexistent. In other words, they know they have power over others, but what they really want is more power over themselves.

The "No-Comeback Point"

Somewhere near or beyond point 5 on the Progression of Deviancy scale, the youngster begins to internalize that any movement back toward acceptable behavior is not reasonable for him ("Why should I," he might say, "it's all their fault anyway") or too difficult to do ("It would be too much work and effort") or, from his perspective, perhaps even impossible ("I can't go back").

Occasionally there are a few youngsters on the very far right end of the Progression of Deviancy who do make it back to permanently acceptable behavior, but there are very few. Of the hundreds of youngsters with Conduct Disorder who I have evaluated over the years for the juvenile justice system, most of them today as adults either have been in jail, are presently in jail, will be going to jail, or are dead. The Tanya Tucker song "It's a Little Too Late to Do the Right Thing Now" unfortunately describes a number of these kids all too well.

It should not come as a surprise, then, that the deviant mirror image of the "good kid" is the youngster with Conduct Disorder, as evidenced by the following characteristics:

Characteristic #1: This youngster has poor social skills. This child usually comes from an environment where social skills have not been modeled. Socially impoverished, ignorant, and indifferent, this child at best is apt to feel that the exercise of appropriate social skills is a sign of weakness, not strength.

Characteristic #2: The child feels that no one cares about him or her. These youngsters are apt to believe that no one really cares about them, not even their own family. As a result, the child doesn't care either. This alone makes change difficult.

Characteristic #3: The youngster is poor in academics. It usually works out that this youngster is behind age and grade peers in academic skills. This is a continual source of embarrassment, frustration, and trouble. In fact, I believe that academic deficiencies are a strong contributor to the development of Conduct Disorder in the first place.

Characteristic #4: Inappropriate behaviors are direct and blatant. It is not at all unusual for this child to have a run-in with the law before the early teens, and an established record with the police by late teens.

Characteristic #5: This youngster craves power. Because of the accumulated consequences of poor social skills and deficient academic ability, this child craves power and control. Since authentic and appropriate power is difficult to obtain, the youngster often resorts to "pseudo-power" through bullying and the physical intimidation of others. These behaviors only lead the child into yet more trouble. The whole process cycles toward yet more and more deviancy.

Not the Same Disorder

Among mental health professionals there are plenty of folks who regard the child with Oppositional Defiant Disorder and the child with Conduct Disorder as being in different developmental stages of the same disorder (Rutter & Shaffer, 1980; Werry, 1987). I obviously do not. There is ample evidence to suggest that not all youngsters with Oppositional Defiant Disorder develop into Conduct Disorder (Cantwell & Baker, 1989; Lahey et al., 1992). The child with Conduct Disorder is not out stealing hubcaps on the day he is born, however. He progresses *through* Oppositional Defiant Disorder, and might even be diagnosed as such at some point. Behavioral deviancy, even Conduct Disorder, takes time to reach serious proportions. Research indicates that about 84% of youngsters with Conduct Disorder *also* demonstrate oppositional and defiant behavior (Spitzer et al., 1990). These particular youngsters are obviously beyond the scope and intent of this book.

It is safe to say that youngsters with Conduct Disorder will usually be oppositional and defiant in behavior, but children with Oppositional Defiant Disorder will not necessarily "cross the line" into Conduct Disorder. Put yet another way, children displaying oppositional and defiant behavior usually have a pretty clear notion of what they will *not* do, including things like running away from home, vandalizing the neighborhood, and terrorizing folks in general. In fact, it is quite likely that many of these youngsters will never even be diagnosed as Oppositional Defiant Disorder—they simply display some of the behaviors. On the other hand, youngsters with Conduct Disorder are apt to do just about *anything*.

In terms of management and intervention, it is important to understand these differences; they are critical in terms of diagnoses and management. It is also helpful to be aware that Oppositional Defiant Disorder and Conduct Disorder have been increasing in numbers of youngsters diagnosed, and in the severity of behaviors manifested by children with these disorders, ever since they were both included in the *Diagnostic and Statistical Manual of Mental Disorders* (APA, 1980, 1987, 1994). Unfortunately, it appears that the numbers will continue to climb.

Chapter Five

Victory by Default

Respond or React?

Human behavior comes in two basic forms—responses and reactions. Most behaviors are responses. They are deliberate. Making a trip to the supermarket whenever the cupboard is bare is an example of a response.

Responses are also under direct control. A person knows that a trip to the supermarket is necessary, but the day and time of the trip, and even the choice of supermarket, are open to the discretion of the shopper.

Persistent oppositional and defiant behaviors are of the response variety. They are deliberate and controlled, although youngsters may not always be completely aware of why they behave as they do (for this reason a direct approach to dealing with this youngster is guaranteed to be both frustrating and fruitless much of the time).

Reactions, although deliberate, are not well controlled. They just happen, often with catastrophic results. The employee who, in a moment of frustration and rage, tosses his office keys at his boss and tells her exactly where she can put her company, runs the risk of later regretting such a maneuver all the way to the unemployment office.

When parents succumb to a barrage of rapid-fire irritation from their oppositional and defiant child, they often react in ways that worsen both the relationship and the behaviors. Fortunately, more effective strategies can be learned.

Victory Just the Same

The choice to do nothing is a stroke of genius. It is the oppositional and defiant youngster's most devastating response. The child wins with this approach by letting the consequences explode all over the parent. Whenever a father says, "You will do this, or else!," Junior opts for "or else," sending Pop's blood pressure right off the scale. The kid wins another one—by default.

But hey, it's victory just the same.

No-lutions

Oppositional and defiant youngsters win because they are *given* a way to win. Adults also provide an incentive in the way they keep cycling through what I call the "No-lutions."

No-lutions are the ways parents futilely try to deal with their oppositional and defiant kids. No-lutions are like solutions, except for one significant difference: No-lutions never *solve* anything. In short, they are no solutions! But in spite of the fact that they can and often do make things worse, No-lutions are used over and over again.

There are seven No-lutions that parents and authority figures typically employ in attempting to manage oppositional and defiant youngsters. They are listed in Figure 5-1. We will examine each of these No-lutions in turn, and see exactly why they don't work.

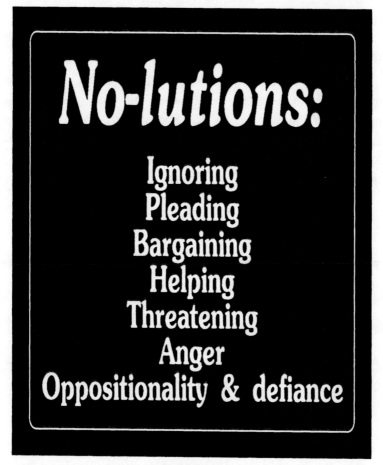

Figure 5-1

No-lution #1: Ignoring. The "I'll just pretend that I don't see it" approach does work sometimes. If the behavior of a youngster who forgets and leaves his bicycle out in the rain can be ignored, the resulting consequence of pedaling rusty transportation comes to bear all on its own.

Of course, there are behaviors we best not ignore. Parents especially cannot afford to ignore a youngster whose behaviors compromise safety and welfare. A mother, for example, can't very well ignore the behavior of the three-year-old who wants to play "chicken" with the traffic.

Why it doesn't work with this kid: Oppositional and defiant youngsters are driven by their own unique agenda. Whenever we try to ignore them, these kids just crank it up a notch. They have to, really, because they don't know whether their slings and arrows are hitting the mark unless we do or say something to let them know. And sooner or later, we usually do.

No-lution #2: Pleading. Pleading with a youngster can be effective even if such a tactic is born of frustration. "Please stop that, you are embarrassing me!" makes an appeal to the relationship. Sometimes it even works.

Why it doesn't work with this kid: It gives the child *precisely* what he wants—control. He has pushed our buttons, and we have acknowledged it. We might as well light up the sky with fireworks.

No-lution #3: Bargaining. Pleading generally turns into bargaining. Everyone is always looking for a better deal. Madison Avenue has fostered this frenzy through prices that mean nothing because everything is perpetually "On Sale!" I know of a person who hated having to pay full price at a fast-food place when he didn't have any discount coupons on him. The "What's-in-it-for-me?" mentality describes everyone to some degree. We think that if we could just up the ante enough, perhaps we could encourage this youngster to do something, or in some cases, *stop* doing it.

Why it doesn't work with this kid: Bargaining serves to keep unacceptable behaviors very close at hand. Think about it. Even though a specific problem might be temporarily solved, the stage is set for more conflict (and more bargaining). Admission to the next hassle has been paid—in full.

There's an old story going around that illustrates this concept, a story about a fisherman, a snake, and a frog. It's a perfect day, and the fisherman is out on the lake in his boat. As he is fishing, something thumps against the side of his boat.

He checks it out, only to discover that the thump was caused by a snake that is grasping a frog in its mouth. Feeling compassion for the unfortunate frog, the fisherman pries open the snake's mouth, removes the frog, and sets it free.

Now the frog is happy, but the snake is miserable. As the fisherman peers into the sad, hungry eyes of the poor snake, he ponders a way to set things straight. But all he has in the boat with him is a bottle of bourbon. So, in a gesture of kindness, he gives the snake a sip or two of the booze and watches him swim off as happily as the frog.

The fisherman returns to his lines, only to be interrupted by another thump, except it's louder than the first. His friend the snake is back—but this time he has *two* frogs!

This little snake learned quickly that the way to load up on bourbon was to be a terror on frogs. This story describes what is probably the oldest behavioral principle on the books, a principle that fits perfectly with our life experience: It is the behaviors that we *reward* that keep thumping on our boat, not the behaviors that we want, hope for, or even plead for.

Ultimately, the No-lution of bargaining can result in a household version of hostage-taking. And guess who's wearing the handcuffs?

Here's a hint—it ain't the kid.

No-lution #4: Helping. Eventually the thought occurs to us that these youngsters might not know *how* to do what we are asking. Perhaps they need just a bit more instruction, a trial run, or just a little boost. Sometimes a hand from the adult is both helpful and appreciated, we keep thinking.

Why it doesn't work with this kid: Oppositional and defiant youngsters never graduated from the Class of the Terrible Twos. As far as they're concerned, they don't *need* your help, and certainly don't *want* your help. Although they might verbally be agreeable to assistance, the resulting behavior usually works against the help offered.

The most classic example of this No-lution in action regards the youngster who is failing to turn in schoolwork.

The teacher and the parents come up with a rather elaborate homework checklist as a way of correcting the problem of the missing assignments.

This thing is a piece of work! It has sections for each class, a place to write the assignments for each day, and places for the initials of the adults involved as the assignments travel from the classroom to home and back. It's surefire and foolproof. Even Johnny himself applauds the strategy.

But the very next thing to disappear is not the homework—it's the checklist.

No-lution #5: Threatening. Threatening is, admittedly, a primitive approach. Although it's not recommended, it has been used for eons. "If you don't stop that this minute, I'm going to _____!" is a pretty clear message that can sometimes put a youngster in gear.

Why it doesn't work with this kid: Just like pleading, threatening exposes enough of our frustration to let the youngster know that he has again gotten into our "button box," and we have reacted. Whenever we use threatening as an intervention we are sending the youngster the crystal-clear message that he has struck a nerve— usually our very last one. The child is probably thinking, "You can tell me you'll take everything away from me, but watching you blow up is *worth* it!"

Here's the scene: We might tell Junior we'll pay him an extra buck if he'll take out the trash and mow the lawn before 4 o'clock. But what we don't tell him is that if he *doesn't* do what we ask, we will give him much more than a dollar's worth of thrills.

Look at it this way. If you were a slightly resistant twelve-year-old, which would *you* rather do—slip a buck in your jeans, or have a live one on the line? It's really a simple game of payoffs.

No-lution #6: Anger. Most youngsters don't want to see folks angry and upset, especially at them. But a little anger, appropriately expressed, can often spur cooperation and clear the air, can't it?

Why it doesn't work with this kid: To this point, no particular No-lution has provided much satisfaction. This is exactly why the next episode from this youngster pushes us slap-dab over the edge.

It is a case of threatening gone to seed, usually with a much bigger payoff. I knew of one bright girl whose father would fly into a rage every time he looked at her ninth-grade report card. "All I want you to do is pass—just pass!" he would scream at her.

This girl is presently in her fourth year as a freshman.

Although it understandably bothers us when we occasionally lose our temper with these youngsters, I believe there is a worse situation. I'm speaking of the adult who is coming apart at the seams, while at the same time internally and verbally denying the fact that he or she is upset at all.

Very early in my own education, I had such an adult in my life—a teacher. She was a thin, frail woman who spent much of her time standing on top of her chair or desk telling us exactly how upset she was *not*.

She would flip the lights on and off, glaring at us over her half-frame spectacles. Then she would fly into us with a voice that would jam radar.

"Class!" I could sense the windows straining not to shatter.

"You all are trying to make me angry. But I will not become angry." The word "But" spewed out upon us like a projectile. She continued.

"So, I have decided that we will just sit here until our AT-TI-TUDE begins to improve." No, she wasn't upset.

Not much, she wasn't!

After anger has run its course, some guilt usually replaces it. After all, this kid hasn't stolen anything or shot anyone. After a bit of calmer reflection, our little episode of outrage seems too extreme, even to us.

We lost it, we know it, and we generally feel bad about it.

No-lution #7: Oppositionality and defiance.
Here's the adult's message (or something very close to it):

> *"Oh, I'm so sorry! I meant to take care of that for you. It just sorta slipped my mind, I guess."*

It is said that running water seeks its own level. Well, here is the equivalent in terms of behavior and interaction within relationships. Although our own oppositional and defiant behavior occasionally works, it is rarely effective over the long haul. It does, however, at least seem fair.

Why it doesn't work with this kid: This youngster is thinking,

> *"I can't believe this! You're doing the same thing you're telling me not to do."*

Such interactions have an innocent beginning and a disastrous end, as in the following example.

Dad makes the first move:

> *"Suzie, look up there, in the fork of that tallest tree. That sure would be a keen place for a treehouse."*

"Oh yeah!" she replies. "Would you help me build one, Daddy?" Chomp—the bait is taken.

"Why sure, honey; I'll check it out," Dad replies, "just as soon as I can get around to it."

This dialogue repeats itself a number of times over the next few months with, of course, no treehouse ever taking shape.

You see, when Dad can "get around to it" has a whole lot to do with when Suzie can "get around to" a few items of Dad's choosing. It turns into a game of double aggravation, with each party trying to deliver the knockout punch. It's no wonder why relationships like this one can take a tumble.

Truth Is Truth

If you are like most parents, the trip through these No-lutions may have left you a bit frustrated. It comes with the territory. I know; I've been there.

Although my intent in this chapter was not to discourage, truth is still truth. Acknowledging it can best lead us to hope and, ultimately, to solutions in working more effectively with the oppositional and defiant youngster.

The next chapter will offer more insight into why these youngsters behave as they do.

If My Kid's So Nice ... Why's He Driving ME Crazy?

Chapter Six

Trouble Under the Table

The Kilmer Syndrome

My daughter has a dog—a Dalmatian named Kilmer. Having never gotten the message that at some point growth stops, Kilmer is now about the size of a small pony. Not content to roam aimlessly in my back yard, Kilmer set out to eat everything that resembled plant life. Upon accomplishing that mission, he started in on the patio furniture.

Whenever I would go out to feed Kilmer and check his water bowl, we played out a ritual. It was always the same. Kilmer would jump up and put his front paws on my chest, then commence licking me in the face. It was Dalmatian, I suppose, for "I love you, Pops." At the very same time that he was giving me the facial, however, Kilmer made it a point to "sprinkle" on my trousers.

What a picture of a mixed message if there ever was one—all that affection upstairs, and all that aggravation downstairs. (It was *my* aggravation, to be sure; the dog was not *intending* to upset me.) I call it the "Kilmer Syndrome." This picture also applies perfectly to the characteristics of the oppositional and defiant child.

Table It

Take the Kilmer Syndrome—the licking, sprinkling dog—and transfer it to a common piece of household furniture like the kitchen table (or, if you prefer, the "Kilmer Table"). Consider Figure 6-1. Above the table there is the "face-licking," represented by those issues and behaviors that are favorable ("I need your affirmation and approval"). Underneath the table, however, lurks what is causing the damp britches, those hidden issues and behaviors that are *not* favorable ("I have trouble and conflict with authority").

As a normal aspect of social growth, we are taught to deal with people in a direct and open fashion. We learn to admire those folks who conduct their business *above* the table. Nothing is hidden, or even needs to be hidden. We admire and respect these folks so much that we've developed expressions such as "Bring your issues to the table," "Put all of your cards *on* the table," and "We should be open and *above*board." We learn to take pride in this ability in ourselves, and we learn that it is best to approach relationships in this manner. It's an approach that allows us a way to deal with the issues and the people who interfere with our needs. It's an honest approach; it works well just about all of the time.

Unfortunately, the oppositional and defiant child is uncomfortable with honesty, sometimes even terrified of it. How can he or she admit their problem with authority (an "under the table" problem) without losing some or all of the affirmation and approval from that authority figure (an "above the table" need)? It puts the child into a bind; I call it the Psycho-Behavioral Bind.

Figure 6-1

Caught in the Bind

An adolescent caught in this bind doesn't say to Mom, "I don't like mashed potatoes when you make them this way." She fears Mom's anger (and rejection) and perhaps even fears the thought of *wearing* the potatoes if Mom becomes really upset with her. Neither does she tell her teacher, "Sometimes you give us too much homework," for fear that she will be chastised and branded as a troublemaker. Instead, she doesn't eat the potatoes and she doesn't complete the homework. This youngster then covers her pain with a smile that says, "Everything is just fine."

But it's *not* fine; of course it's not. The adults are still upset, although confused, and the girl is also upset. Underneath the table she piles plenty of hurt on top of humiliation, and rage on top of resentment. Since this stuff is shoved *under* the table (and concealed behind a cover), it is simply not available for discussion. It sits there, simmering, bubbling, and stewing, like steam testing a pressure cooker.

Occasionally it boils over—to the astonishment of those who only saw the smile.

The Challenge

The challenge of effectively relating to the oppositional and defiant child or adolescent is to discuss and work through the conflicts that are *under* the table without causing the youngster to become fearful of losing what is *above* the table, our affirmation and approval.

If this challenge seems like a difficult one, it certainly can be. These youngsters can become so guarded in their interactions with parents and other authority figures that they will *insist* there is no problem. This is why traditional counseling and direct approaches to getting at the issues so often produce more heat than light. This is the reason why years of counseling, at the cost of a great deal of money, too often result in precious little change.

Emotional safety for the child, therefore, is the issue. This youngster must feel that it is *safe* to speak about things that bring discomfort. The next chapter discusses how one family accomplished this task.

Chapter Seven

The Quick Fix

It is entirely possible to resolve difficulty with the oppositional and defiant youngster in a relatively short period of time, sometimes in a matter of hours. That's the good news. The bad news is that it rarely happens, not because it is especially difficult, but because *people* can be so difficult.

With Luke, the "cure" was both quick and permanent.

Luke

Years ago a friend read some materials that I had prepared for a teacher/counselor training session. She was amazed to discover that my description of the oppositional and defiant child fit her eighth-grade son perfectly.

Luke was a strong student, but failure to complete classwork had earned him "D's" in two classes. My friend and her husband had threatened to take the boy out of basketball if he didn't immediately begin to bring up his grades (this was a few years before the "No Pass, No Play" rule came into effect in Texas schools).

Luke called his parents' bluff, saying that he really doubted they would embarrass him or cause him to become depressed if he were removed from sports. And besides, wasn't it Dad who really wanted him to play in the first place?

The young man was right.

Mom asked me what they should do. Knowing this family, I suggested a super-shortcut. I added that it was an easy one to recommend, but quite another story to implement. She assured me that, whatever it took, they were going to get through to their boy.

The "Quick Fix" Formula

When it comes to the issue of healing, I don't speak lightly of cures; no one should. And yet Luke's parents certainly considered this simple "formula" to be nothing short of a miracle from the changes, permanent changes, it produced (the formula is summarized in Figure 7-1).

I gave Mom the formula. I encouraged her and her husband to set aside some time for a discussion with Luke. I suggested they begin by sharing with the boy that failure in capable youngsters is often a type of "message" to one or both parents about resentment, and that knowing the problem is an important part of resolving it. I added that they should communicate to the boy their desire to change also, if needed.

I told Mom it was important that they clearly let the youngster know that their love and affirmation were not at stake. He should be encouraged to speak freely, with the understanding that it would not be held against him.

Finally, I told Mom to be patient. The truth might be very difficult for the boy to identify and share. With patience, however, the truth should come.

The "Quick Fix" Formula

Communicate to the child that:

1. There seems to be a connection between the "problem" and resentment toward authority.
2. You could also be part of the "problem," and are willing to change.
3. There is no penalty for being honest.
4. You'll be patient.

Figure 7-1

I saw her the next morning, a bit bleary-eyed, but obviously pleased. She related how she and her husband sat down with Luke at about 7:00 p.m., and told him that they really wanted to know what was bothering him. To this question he immediately replied, "Nothing—nothing is the matter" (denial *is* the first response).

But they stayed with it. At a few minutes past 11:00 p.m., Luke blurted out, "I'm sorry, Dad. If you really gotta know, I just can't stand it whenever you yell at me!"

Dad was shocked—and hurt. But he handled it like a trooper. Much to his credit for the ultimate healing that followed, Dad put *his* feelings aside and focused on his son. His response:

> *"Son, what you said hits me like a shot. I thank you for telling me, though, because I very much needed to hear it. Luke, you are more important to me than life itself. I would never deliberately do anything to hurt you. I cannot promise you that I will never again raise my voice at you, but now that you have made me aware of it, I will certainly work on it. Son, I am deeply sorry, and I ask for your forgiveness."*

Luke's forgiveness of his father was swift and genuine. A relationship was repaired in less than five minutes. Grades and schoolwork, as well as compliance in even doing chores around the house, improved overnight. It was as if a miracle had taken place.

The Real Miracle

The real miracle in this family story was Dad's exceptional willingness to take a risk and put some genuine caring ahead of his own needs to direct and control. In this case it paid off. In a paradoxical sort of way, Dad's ability to put Luke's needs ahead of what he himself wanted enabled Dad to get *exactly* what he wanted. He gave a little, but he gained everything.

Contrast Dad's response and its favorable outcome to what Dad *could* have said:

> *"What? How dare you talk to me like that (screaming)! I wouldn't **have** to raise my voice if you weren't so intent on sending your mother and me to an early grave. It's **your fault, all** of it."*

Such a response, or one similar to it, would be common. It would totally obliterate the second and third parts of the formula (being willing to change and encouraging an honest response by assuring Luke of their love and regard for him), probably ensuring that the youngster would think twice about *ever* being honest about his feelings again. And, of course, the problems at school would have continued. No one would have won, not even Luke.

Why It Worked

Luke's folks made a great deal of progress with their son that night for the following reasons (summarized in Figure 7-2):

Reason #1: They demonstrated that they cared about Luke. Although Luke already knew that his folks loved him, their restatement to him of their affection was important.

Reason #2: They were patient. Today it's almost unheard of that a set of parents would spent four hours trying to reach a defiant son or daughter. Most would have given up long before 11:00 p.m.

Reason #3: The issue seemed to be an isolated one. In other words, there was not a lot of excess emotional baggage that had been piling up over the years. In spite of the fact that Luke really didn't like it whenever his father raised his voice at him, there were positive things going on in the relationship.

Reason #4: They were willing to make themselves vulnerable. No one wants to admit they made a mistake, but those who can will enjoy better relationships. They will also sleep better at night.

Reason #5: They considered Luke's needs before their own. In the long run, this is probably the main reason why the boy finally voiced the problem. When parents are in conflict with a child, it is very difficult at times to put the youngster's needs first. The rewards are excellent, however, for those parents who can actually do it.

Why Luke's Parents Were Successful

1. They demonstrated that they cared.

2. They were patient.

3. There were not many unresolved issues.

4. They made themselves vulnerable.

5. They focused on Luke's needs.

Figure 7-2

Change *Is* Possible

For certain, turnaround stories like Luke's are much more the exception than the rule. But so are folks like Luke and his parents.

Parents, and even teachers and counselors, of youngsters like Luke (and Doug, Linda, and Kevin from Chapter One) should take heart. Change *is* possible, although it usually takes a bit longer. The next chapter will focus on elements of adult-child relationships that must be in place for change to work.

Chapter Eight

Expectations

Children value and need meaningful and productive relationships with adults in their lives. Even during adolescence, youngsters never really outgrow their need for an adult friend or mentor, someone who can help them try the world on for size.

Such adults are special indeed. They come in all kinds, colors, and ages, and they love young people. Additionally, they hold two attributes in common. First of all, they know how to guide youngsters with their wisdom instead their muscle. Secondly, they know how to project this wisdom with a sense of unselfish caring for the youngster. Young people are aware of these qualities, and they actively search for these adults. Sometimes they find them; sometimes they don't.

"Special" Adults

In studying adults and young people who have a common attraction, I have found that they have a rather pure and uncomplicated relationship. Figure 8-1 is a model of this sort of interaction. Both adult and child benefit in this friendship, and the relationship flourishes without need for expectations. Oh, I suppose one could make a case that even this relationship contains *some* expectations, but they would be minimal in light of the other benefits of the relationship.

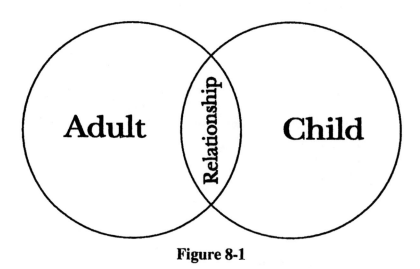

Figure 8-1

A thought. Of necessity, the adult who has the relationship with the child in Figure 8-1 is usually not the one accountable for the life and welfare of the youngster. Such a responsibility *would* involve expectations, so it is generally true that the adult in the figure would *not* be the child's parent or teacher. This would especially be the case if the youngster happened to be resistant by nature. In terms of expectations, we could describe the relationship in Figure 8-1 as "unconditional." This unconditionality applies to all of the interaction between the special adult and the child. It contains spontaneity and fun. For me, that adult in my early years was my grandmother.

My mother's parent, Myrtle Smith, was a "double duty" grandmother because my father's mother passed away before I was born. Since I was the only grandchild for several years on my mother's side, Grandma and I developed a closeness that grew and deepened until her death in 1968. When she died, I lost more than my grandmother; I lost a dear friend. Later, I again shared this kind of relationship with a man who owned the radio station in my hometown. In concert with my own mother and father, these individuals had a hand in shaping my life.

Rarely does the adult "friend" in Figure 8-1 ever encounter behavior problems with the child. There just aren't any places for conflict to grab a toehold.

Parents and Teachers

The model in Figure 8-2 depicts the adult-child interaction whenever *expectations* come into play. This certainly does not mean that expectations are bad. Society *expects* parents to feed, clothe, protect, and nurture their young. In fact, powerful laws are built around these expectations. In like fashion, educators are *expected* to teach social harmony and impart wisdom and knowledge, while at the same time ensuring the safety and welfare of the youngsters they serve.

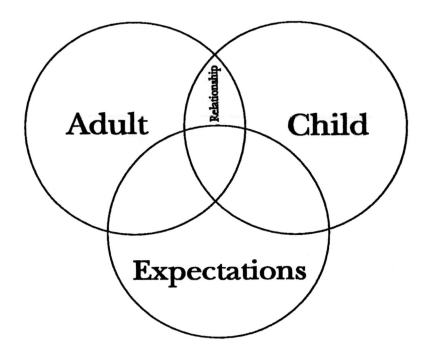

Figure 8-2

Children are not exempt from expectations. It is expected that they will honor the authority of their parents and be compliant at school.

Observe that, although expectations consume a large part of the interaction between the adult and the child, there is still a relationship in Figure 8-2 that, like the adult-child relationship in Figure 8-1, remains unconditional and spontaneous. Even though this relationship is smaller by comparison, both the adult and the child are able to thrive and grow in it. *It is important that this relationship be*

- 80 -

there. Luke's parents (in the previous chapter) focused on this unconditional relationship in their discussion with their son. As a result, things improved, and improved quickly.

It is not only possible, but necessary, for parents to occasionally activate an unconditional role with their child. When they play with their youngster, or seem genuinely interested in the child's thoughts and feelings, they make it easy for the youngster to respond to their support. This relationship can indeed become a breath of fresh air during an otherwise long, hard journey through childhood and adolescence. For the youngster, not ever experiencing this unconditional parent-child or teacher-child relationship would be like going to school for twelve or thirteen years without *ever* having a summer off. At best it would be miserable—and oppositionality and defiance flourish in a bed of misery.

More Than Friends

It is easy sometimes to confuse Figure 8-1 and Figure 8-2 interactions. A number of years ago, I shared the platform with another psychologist; we were training educators. He stepped up to the lectern and said, "We could solve many of our problems with our children if we just treated them as we would treat our very best friend."

I do admit that it sounded good. In application, however, to follow such advice would be foolish and absurd. Our children are *not* our friends, they are our children. There *is* a difference.

The only real "glue" that holds friendships together is a bond of agreement. It is possible to lose contact with a friend for months, even years, then rejuvenate that bond quickly with a bit of time and effort. If parents check out of a relationship with their children for that amount of time, however, the results can be devastating.

The interaction illustrated in Figure 8-2 contains balance. Expectations are there, as they should be, but there is also a comparable amount of unconditional respect, deep interest and concern, honesty, and open communication. Both the adult and the child benefit from the experience.

The Core of the Problem

Two statements from this chapter stand out as significant observations:

Statement #1: Rarely does the adult "friend" in Figure 8-1 ever encounter behavior problems with the child.

Statement #2: Oppositionality and defiance flourish in a bed of misery.

These statements are tied together by the issue of *expectations*. For the oppositional and defiant child, expectations represent the core of the problem; but fortunately, they also represent the most direct route to solutions and change.

Figure 8-3 could easily involve an oppositional and defiant child. Do you see the problem? Almost *everything* is conditional ("I love you and I affirm you whenever you _____"). These adults are apt to say to the child, "I just want you to be happy." Then they produce a long list they have prepared, saying, "Now, here's how you're going to be happy." Expectations have just about completely choked out the unconditional relationship (even the word "relationship" in the figure is essentially unreadable).

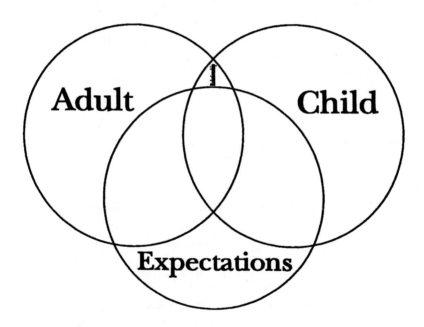

Figure 8-3

Insight and Change

In their simplicity, these three models, Figures 8-1, 8-2, and 8-3, contain the seeds for change. As parents we are often willing to change *if* we can clearly see the problem and have the insight, courage, and commitment to do whatever it takes to realize improvement.

This is not to say it is easy to reduce excessive expectations and increase unconditional relationships with our children—especially if we deeply feel that our expectations represent part of what we must require of our children in order to remain decent and responsible parents. Besides, there are those expectations that are simply not negotiable, such as "I expect you to be a law-abiding citizen."

The well-intended act of assessing and adjusting expectations does work, as evidenced by these words shared with me by a clinical psychologist in New Mexico following a workshop I had conducted there.

> *"I used the concept of the overlapping circles with one mother. She is now listening more and judging less, and is being more introspective. Her daughter is finding her way back to school and is completing homework more readily. It's always nice to hear experience coupled with expertise, insight, and a practical approach."*

Four Questions

I encourage you to take this four-question test. See if *you're* ready to take some responsibility for lasting change.

Question #1: Am I being excessive in my expectations of my son or daughter?

Question #2: Do some of these expectations lose their value in light of the damage they could do to the relationship?

Question #3: Do I spend most of my one-on-one time with this child discussing *my* expectations?

Question #4: Am I willing to ease up on some of my expectations if I believe it will help the relationship?

Note: In answering "Yes" to any of these questions, I understand that I will not do, or be asked to do, anything that would conflict with my values or my intention to be a responsible parent.

If My Kid's So Nice ... Why's He Driving ME Crazy?

Chapter Nine

Three Reasons Why

Persistent oppositional and defiant behavior in young people is usually attributable to one of three reasons: the disposition of the child; excessive expectations; or some sort of emotional or psychological distress (also listed in Figure 9-1).

Disposition of the Child

In other words, that's just the way the kid is. I was in the psychology business for years before I realized that some youngsters were oppositional and defiant on the day they were born. The doctor held them by their heels in the delivery room, swatted them on the fanny—and they refused to cry. It's been struggle, struggle, struggle ever since.

Disposition implies that, in general, nothing *outside* of the youngster has provoked the oppositional and defiant behavior (although, given time, those in authority will certainly begin to react to this child in predictable ways).

The focus of understanding and managing this youngster is built around the notion that this is a healthy and otherwise normally functioning child (youngsters who are sick or otherwise handicapped will be discussed in the next chapter).

This oppositional and defiant child could come from a home where every other sibling is reasonable and compliant, and where the parenting skills of the mother and father have been effective with every child but *this* one.

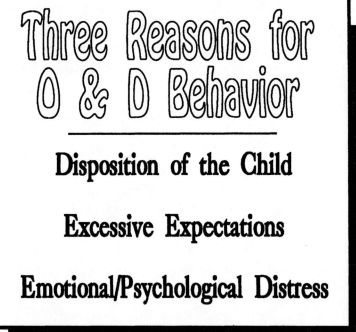

Three Reasons for O & D Behavior

Disposition of the Child

Excessive Expectations

Emotional/Psychological Distress

Figure 9-1

Excessive Expectations

As addressed in the previous chapter, excessive expectations and the choking out of choices can evoke oppositional and defiant behavior. As will be addressed in Chapter Eleven, it is the child's perspective of the situation, not the actual reality of relationships and events, that brings out the behavior.

It is interesting to note that the *Diagnostic and Statistical Manual of Mental Disorders IV* ,(APA, 1994) contains four pages about the oppositional and defiant child. This finding stands in sharp contrast to the 1968 edition of the same document (*DSM-II*), which contained no category at all for this same child. In my opinion, this dramatic difference across twenty-six years is connected to a group we call the Baby Boomers.

Characteristically, the Boomers (born between 1946 and 1964) currently hold much of our nation's wealth, influence, power, and leadership. They are used to having their way with things. More often than not, their white-collar lifestyles sprouted from blue-collar roots. Many oppositional and defiant youngsters are children or grandchildren of the Boomers. These young people, the Boomers' Kids, are scattered throughout the educational process from kindergarten to grad school.

The Boomers and the Boomers' Kids were, for all practical purposes, brought up on different planets, where rules, expectations, and the whole concept of attainable success were simply not the same. As a result there have been problems.

The Boomers came into this world on the wings of exceptional opportunity, opportunity created by world circumstance. World War II and the Korean Conflict were over, and folks went about the business of carving out a piece of the American Dream for themselves and their offspring. They were aided by cheap gasoline, cheap groceries, cheap payments, and parents who had paved the way.

I arrived thirteen months before the first official Boomer, but I did marry one, and we were both around for the pickings. Our first home, three bedrooms with brick trim, cost us less than $17,000 total (today a mid-size automobile will cost you that or more). The GI Bill carried me through to my doctorate. Insurance was affordable, and benefits were outstanding (it cost us less than $2 to take our firstborn home from the hospital).

In pursuing their goals and ideals, the Boomers moved ahead of the income and lifestyles of their parents, but without much pressure to do so. Today, many of them are first-generation college graduates. This has been a source of great pride to their parents (I'm sharing a bit of my own story here), but again, there was little pressure on them. And yet, the Boomers, especially the older ones, can still recall elements of the "Good Old Days," like gas space heaters, black-and-white TV (only!), and clothes that *always* had to be ironed.

In terms of admonitions and expectations, the Boomers have instructed their children to follow the trail that they had blazed. "Do at least as well as we have—better if you can" could be their not-so-subtle message. From piano lessons to karate classes, from cheerleader tryouts to first-string football, the expectations have been oppressive and quite high—sometimes painfully, painfully high.

For the Boomers' Kids, the bar has been raised. It will be very difficult, and dangerously close to impossible in some cases, for the Boomers' Kids to match the accomplishments of their folks. The heat is on. Things have changed that much in the course of just one generation.

The results? There is a type of silent rebellion (and sometimes not so silent) against the demands, expectations, and excessive strictness of parents and other forms of authority. This strife between parents and children has been substantiated in research for some time now (Levy, 1955; Meeks, 1979; Gard & Berry, 1986). These kids learn how to activate their rebellion in a manner that is truly ingenious and "safe." They do nothing at all. The tougher the expectations and mandates, the more nothing they do!

Without better intervention, strategies, and attention to the essence of family relationships and interaction, I don't see things changing all that much.

Emotional/Psychological Distress

Since this reason involves distress that is placed upon the child from the *outside*, it is the exact opposite of the first reason mentioned (the disposition that is *inside* the child). Emotional and psychological distress break down into two categories: Acute and Chronic.

Acute Distress. Included here are situational losses, especially those losses that could represent a crisis for the child. These include such "normal" events as moving, prolonged hospitalization, the death of a loved one, divorce, and, in the case of young children, even the loss of a beloved pet. More stressful events might include accidents, severe bouts of nature (floods, tornados, fires, and hurricanes forceful enough to destroy homes and lives), and intentional harm, such as drive-by shootings.

All of these stressful situations can substantially impact a child's emotional balance and psychological state. The youngster is forced to make abrupt and unacceptable changes to life's negative circumstances and events.

Part of the natural recovery process is the regaining of personal control over one's life. In recovering from the initial trauma, youngsters eventually reach a point where they attempt, through behavior, to protect themselves from ever being as vulnerable again. Oppositional and defiant behavior is often the way they attempt to protect themselves. After a crisis event, if a child exhibits oppositional and defiant behavior that was not there *before* the crisis event, this behavior can be viewed as evidence of emotional progress back toward a state of normal functioning. The good news is that this "situational" kind of oppositional and defiant behavior is generally temporary in nature.

An excellent reference for working with the crisis-affected child is *Children of Crisis, Violence, and Loss* (Sutton, 1995). This book, also available through Friendly Oaks Publications, was written with a sensitivity to the unique behaviors of children and adolescents who are under acute distress. It contains a number of helpful strategies and interventions that are built around the twenty most significant challenges of working with crisis-affected youngsters.

Chronic Distress. This distress is more subtle, more diffuse, and significantly more damaging in terms of long-term consequences. Really extreme examples include physical, sexual, and psychological abuse, as well as abandonment. A home where these things are going on is knocked out of balance by a primary caregiver who is dysfunctional in terms of physical, psychological, or emotional health (McMahon & Forehand, 1984). Doug and Kevin in Chapter One both came from such homes. At least one of the parents had been treated for alcoholism.

Less extreme, but certainly important, would be difficulties with basic temperament in one or both of the parents. If a parent has difficulty tolerating frustration (especially the frustration caused by an oppositional and defiant child), the effective intervention and management of the child's behavior will suffer.

Chronically distressed youngsters, like the acutely distressed ones, are also crisis-affected, but the *precise* crisis that affected them cannot be identified. For these children, life itself is one ongoing crisis.

Sometimes a youngster's oppositional and defiant behavior is heavily influenced by a condition or characteristic that is *within* the child, such as learning deficits, physical disabilities, Attention-Deficit Disorder, and depression. These will be addressed in the next chapter.

If My Kid's So Nice ... Why's He Driving ME Crazy?

Chapter Ten

ADD and Other Things

In this chapter we're going to look at other conditions and disorders that can be associated with or confused with oppositional and defiant behavior, especially with Oppositional Defiant Disorder (ODD). Unlike the externally influenced emotional and psychological distress discussed in the previous chapter, the conditions and disorders in this chapter typically have their beginning *within* the child.

In a study of fifteen boys and thirteen girls diagnosed with ODD, twenty-two of them had other diagnoses as well (Wenning et al., 1993). This works out to a whopping 79%, a figure that cannot be ignored. The "other diagnoses" that will be addressed in this chapter include Attention-Deficit Disorder (ADD), depression, giftedness, disabilities, medical conditions, and psychological disorders (as listed in Figure 10-1). This is by no means an exhaustive list; there are others, I'm sure.

Other conditions/disorders that can be associated with or confused with Oppositional Defiant Disorder:

ADD (ADHD)

Depression

Giftedness

Disabilities

Medical Conditions

Psychological Disorders

Figure 10-1

At first glance, some will perhaps suggest that ADD and depression belong under the category of psychological disorders. No argument there. I have elected to keep them separate, however, because they both profoundly affect the way we interpret Oppositional Defiant Disorder, and because ADD and depression are both conditions that can, and do, exist for years without ever being formally diagnosed as disorders.

ADD (ADHD)

Regarding disorders of childhood, no recent term comes even remotely close to receiving as much press as ADD—Attention-Deficit Disorder. Also referred to as Attention-Deficit/Hyperactivity Disorder (ADHD), the condition is often confused with, and sometimes occurs simultaneously with, Oppositional Defiant Disorder. It's as if they were automatically interchangeable, but they are not. In terms of observed behaviors, there are excellent reasons why these two disorders are confused, although the two conditions can be characteristically very different.

By way of an example, consider a sick child who is running a fever. There are any number of circumstances and diseases that could cause it. Focusing on the fever alone doesn't help the physician much in diagnosing the illness that caused it. In like fashion, both ADD and ODD present similar behaviors, such as "forgetting," disorganization, and poor, sloppy, or incomplete work. Research on simultaneous diagnoses (comorbidity) of ODD and ADD in the same child is at best unclear. Depending on the study, comorbidity of ODD and ADD ranged from 20% to 93% (Rey et al., 1988; Spitzer et al., 1990; Biederman et al., 1991; Pelham, 1992). My own twenty-plus years of experience in working with these youngsters support the lower figures—precisely because both conditions present similar behaviors (although for vastly different reasons). There will be plenty of those who disagree with me. And that's fine; they're certainly free to write their own book.

A Hot Topic. ADD is a red-hot topic. In fact, it has been referred to as America's #1 Childhood Psychiatric Disorder (Hancock, 1996). There are three primary categories of symptoms of the disorder, although not all need apply to any one child. These include impulsivity, poor attention and concentration, and hyperactivity.

Impulsivity is the behavior of acting out (or blurting out) before thinking out. This behavior can spell trouble quickly.

Difficulty with attention and concentration affect both the quality and the quantity of tasks and assignments at school. At home, the completion of chores is hindered by the youngster's difficulty in staying with a task until it is completed.

The presence of hyperactivity, sometimes referred to as "hyperkinesis," puts the child with ADHD in what appears to be perpetual motion. It seems that this kid is never completely still. Hyperactivity is especially a concern whenever it is combined with impulsivity.

ADD is neither "caught" nor "taught," nor is it a consequence of poor parenting. Most professionals feel that it is not related much to diet, although it seems that severe nutritional difficulties could certainly make it worse. ADD is a brain-related neurological condition that is considered to be a problem of development—a type of immaturity.

Medication. Medically, ADD is treated with a stimulant, usually Ritalin (generic name: methylphenidate). The purpose of this medicine is to stimulate the sluggish control part of the brain so that the youngster can better control behavior, concentrate while handling distraction, and think before acting out impulsively.

Many child service professionals, myself included, feel that ADD is being underevaluated, overdiagnosed, and overmedicated in this country. Tremendous increases in the use of Ritalin support this opinion. The Drug Enforcement Administration reported that the use of this medication tripled between 1990 and 1994 (Hancock, 1996). The United States consumes five times more of the stuff than the whole rest of the world combined!

These figures should concern us. From these facts, I can only come to one of two conclusions: Either (1) ADD has actually increased in proportion to the use of the medication (but because the disorder is developmental, not contracted, this is not likely—not in only four years, anyway); or (2) we are diagnosing *other* disorders and conditions as ADD (including depression, anxiety, severe allergies, hearing handicaps, and of course ODD).

Ritalin is classified as an amphetamine—a controlled substance that is in the same category as cocaine, morphine, and methamphetamines. It works well, very well, with the child having ADD, but it won't "fix" the youngster having ODD. Are there youngsters with ODD out there who are being diagnosed and treated as ADD? Absolutely. These youngsters on Ritalin will still have ODD, but they'll be having it in a higher gear!

The solution to this problem is a rather simple one—the careful and comprehensive evaluation and treatment of ADD that is conducted by a team made up of parents, teachers, school support personnel, psychologists, psychiatrists, speech and hearing specialists, and others.

ODD vs. ADD. In contrast to the child with Attention-Deficit Disorder (ADD), the youngster with Oppositional Defiant Disorder (ODD) is considered to have a psychological/emotional condition rather than a physiological/neurological one. ODD is more situational than chronic and ongoing. Finally, ODD responds not so much to medication (although it could be one aspect of treatment in some cases), but to improvements in relationships (which has been the whole focus and intent of this book).

There are a few exceptions, and these are critical. Since ADD is a physical condition, a child having ODD *could* also have ADD (comorbidity), just as he or she could have asthma, diabetes, or any other chronic physical condition. Because of the negativity that ADD brings from others ("Just sit down and be quiet" or "Would you just try to pay attention?"), resulting behavior problems can surface—especially ODD. These behaviors, coming from a youngster with ADD, can look just like ODD because, indeed, they are the *same* behaviors. This is how a psychological/situational disorder can "grow" from a neurological one.

ADD is considered to be a condition that a child is predisposed to develop (similar in many ways to congenital conditions and disorders). For this reason, ADD is generally viewed as a more primary and predisposing condition than ODD. In other words, the child with ADD is more likely to later be diagnosed with ODD than the child with ODD is to be later diagnosed with ADD.

Depression

Entire books can be written on depression, and have been. Any youngster can become depressed, and for a number of reasons. Low-grade depression is common in children and adolescents with ODD, with girls typically presenting twice the rate of depression as boys (Wenning et al., 1993).

In my work with depressed youngsters who have ODD, I have noted three characteristics that seem to appear over and over again:

Characteristic #1: The depression, although usually present to some degree, is either denied or heavily minimized. Even a young child old enough to understand depression ("I feel sad") also knows that it must have a cause. For youngsters with ODD, causes are too painful to examine. To talk about cause is to risk emotional "exposure," thus the denial and minimization.

Characteristic #2: The youngster generally doesn't look depressed. Diagnostically it is easy to overlook in the youngster who is trying to cover it up.

Characteristic #3: To some degree anxiety is also present.

The assessment of depression and anxiety in oppositional and defiant children requires great skill on the part of a psychologist, psychiatrist, counselor, or therapist. Experience doesn't hurt either.

Fortunately, the strategies that are provided here for working more effectively with the oppositional and defiant child will also serve to address depression and anxiety. In extreme cases, the additional assistance of medication is recommended. This is, of course, the responsibility of a physician familiar with childhood diseases and disorders.

Giftedness

Obviously, giftedness isn't really a disorder or a condition, but it can create concern. Many times the brightest kid in the classroom has the most difficulty completing schoolwork and other tasks.

"He's bored!" is a common diagnosis of parents and teachers. The child is then stepped up to the challenges of Gifted and Talented classes and programming.

And he bombs there too. Since the causes of the behavior are not addressed, nothing changes.

Disabilities

Physical Disabilities. The youngster who uses a wheelchair, or who has a physical disability that prevents him from participating with classmates in activities like P.E., is too often reminded that he is different from the others. This is not to say that these youngsters do not adjust. Many do very well, and shine so much in other areas, such as art, music, or writing, that they make a place for themselves among their peers.

There are those youngsters, however, who use their disability to a selfish advantage. "I just can't do that," they might say, or "I'm much too tired to even try it." When defiant behavior begins to hide behind the physical disability, it's much more difficult to pick out.

Sensory Disabilities. Youngsters with visual or hearing impairments can sometimes present a rather complicated picture in terms of behavior. Oppositionality and defiance can easily be disguised ("I can't see what you're asking me to do," or "I don't understand what you're saying"). When the youngster attempts to use a real handicap as a screen for subtle aggression, separating disability from "I ain't gonna" becomes tough.

Years ago, back in the days when oppositional and defiant behavior was called "passive aggression," I saw a classical example of a youngster who was trying to convince her teacher that she was hearing impaired. She was not. She wanted to continue playing with a stack of study cards.

"Put the cards back in the box, Mary," the teacher said.

Mary looked questioningly at her teacher.

"Put the cards away." The teacher pointed to the cards, then to the box.

Mary furrowed her brow, the cards *still* in her hand.

"The cards—put them in the box!" Now the teacher was gesturing wildly as she spoke, as if the girl had suddenly gone stone deaf.

This little scene continued until the teacher, obviously frustrated and shaken, reached over for the cards and put them away herself. Mary had chalked up another one in her "I win!" column.

Learning Disabilities. When we already know that a youngster has a disability with reading, writing, or mathematics, the child can easily disguise refusal or plain old-fashioned laziness behind comments like "I just don't get it." The secret to working effectively with these children is not so much determining where ability ends and inappropriate behavior begins, but rather encouraging them to do their best work most of the time.

Ongoing Medical Conditions

Asthma, leukemia, Tourette's Syndrome, diabetes, and even allergies are just a few childhood diseases and conditions that can seriously affect all aspects of everyday functioning for a child. Additionally, they can affect psychological and emotional functioning as well.

Although I have worked with youngsters having each of the conditions mentioned here, the one category I have found to have the most oppositional and defiant behavior is the child with diabetes. Two such youngsters stand out in my memory.

I first met Marty when I was working part-time for a school district as a speech therapist. Though he was only a first or second grader, Marty's folks and the school nurse encouraged him to take his own glucometer readings, prepare his own insulin, and administer his own injection. Not being on friendly terms with hypodermic syringes, I found the whole scene uncomfortable. I admired Marty for taking on this responsibility at such a young age, but I saw one tremendous behavioral side effect. Marty was the most caustic, belligerent, and uncooperative youngster I had *ever* taught. He had taken oppositional and defiant behavior to a whole new level.

A dozen years or so later I happened to meet Marty at a wedding reception. He appeared to be in excellent health, and the verbal belligerence seemed to be gone—at least in our brief conversation. I did find out, however, that he did not do all that well in his first year of college, and that he had been in the hospital several times due to complications with the diabetes. Apparently, the hospitalizations came as a result of poor attention to his diabetic condition.

Mary was a sixth grader. She lived in a group facility for children because her visually impaired mother had several severe health problems. In fact, Mary and her siblings lived in fear of getting the call that their mother had died from a combination of diabetes, total kidney failure, and abuse of alcohol. The father was in prison for sexual abuse of children, which included Mary. The child was not doing well in school, and she often presented an "attitude." Like Marty, Mary was responsible for taking regular glucometer readings and measuring out and administering her own insulin. Her housemother discovered that Mary had tried to "hide" some of her glucose readings on the glucometer, some of which exceeded 400—with no insulin treatment at all!

I'm convinced that both Marty and Mary desperately wanted to ignore the fact that they had a condition that would be a part of their lives forever; and really, who could blame them? Their bitterness, depression, and resentment spilled over into their behaviors.

Psychological Disorders

The two examples provided here are rare, but they do show how oppositional and defiant behavior can co-exist with another disorder.

Selective Mutism. This disorder describes the child who just doesn't talk in social situations. He or she is capable of speaking, and sometimes will speak to just a friend or two, but not in the classroom or in group social settings. Basically, Selective Mutism (formerly Elective Mutism) could be described as a special variety of oppositional and defiant behavior.

This disorder is an especially frustrating one for teachers to handle. They often find themselves talking to this child as if he had gone deaf or brain-dead. In my whole career I have worked with only one child who had all the characteristics of Selective Mutism (as contrasted to the very shy youngster who will talk, but in a barely audible whisper). For me, one was quite enough.

Severe Eating Disorders. A child who stubbornly refuses to eat his carrots and peas might frustrate the dickens out of his parents, but he will survive to frustrate them yet another day. Severe eating disorders like Anorexia Nervosa (more common in female adolescents and young adult women), however, represent oppositional and defiant behavior with high stakes. The youngster refuses to eat, much to the chagrin of her family. Unfortunately, the begging and pleading of the parents and family only serve to provide enough payoff to set the disorder in concrete. In severe cases, the youngster might lose so much body weight that she has to be fed through a tube—just to keep her alive.

With this disorder, death *is* a possibility. Prompt and competent psychiatric assistance should be sought.

If My Kid's So Nice ... Why's He Driving ME Crazy?

Chapter Eleven

All in the Way You Look at It

To a great extent, oppositional and defiant youngsters are "different" in their perspectives. They often view the very same reality differently from their peers, teachers, and parents, and it can have a profound impact upon their behavior. To really have a grasp of the behavior and how and why it develops, one must be willing to consider the issue of perspective.

A few years ago a Gary Larson cartoon caught my eye. (How would you like to have taught *him* in the fourth grade?) It depicted a scene inside a movie theater. In the audience were families of every kind of bug and insect that you can imagine. They had their popcorn and everything. I'm figuring that the stinkbugs had their *own* section. As the lights dimmed, the title of the movie flashed upon the screen—*Return of the Killer Windshield.*

Perspective—in one simple cartoon Larson nailed it. It's the way we see ourselves, the physical world, and the behaviors and intentions of others. In short, perspective is the color of the glasses that we all wear in examining the world around us. That color is different for each of us, but in its uniqueness, that color spreads its tint over everything that we see—everything.

Not the Same. Perspective and reality are *not* the same. Two individuals can share the same reality, yet have vastly different perspectives. Consider two individuals taking a ride down Space Mountain at Disney World in Florida. One person finds the experience exhilarating; he's ready to go again. The other is terrified, finishing off the experience with a Maalox cocktail. For both, the reality is identical—*exactly* the same. The perspectives, however, are light-years apart.

A small child slips into her parents' bedroom in the middle of the night. She is looking for protection and soothing from the thunderstorm that has frightened her. From her perspective, she is being threatened by the storm, and no amount of reasoning can convince her otherwise. Anyone who has ever tried to comfort a trembling three-year-old during a thunderstorm can remember how fruitless it is to attempt to calm these fears with the words, "Oh honey, there's *nothing* to be afraid of." Right.

Four Perspectives

From what I've been able to gather, the oppositional and defiant youngster clings tightly to at least four perspectives (listed in Figure 11-1). These are critical; and understanding them is important. Since the youngster's behavior comes from these perspectives, influencing changes in them is the first step in realizing improvement in this child's behavior.

Perspectives of the O & D Youngster

I am affirmed only for what I do.

Nothing I ever do is quite good enough.

Just suffer with a smile.

Never let down your guard.

Figure 11-1

Perspective #1: "I am affirmed only for what I do." This perspective views approval and affirmation as always conditional ("I'll be proud of you, Son, *if* you make varsity football—even prouder *if* you're a starter," or "It would really be something *if* you got selected for the dance team"). The youngster feels that, with regard to significant adults in his or her life, all affirmation is based on performance.

Perspective #2: "Nothing I ever do is quite good enough." A youngster brings home a 97 on an important test, and Dad says, "Pretty good, but that one careless mistake right there cost you a 100. You should be more careful." Even when the child does bring home a 100, he or she might hear, "Well, you should be doing this *all* the time." The child doesn't see any way out of this performance trap.

Perspective #3: "Just suffer with a smile." Misery, unhappiness, and suffering are not things that we choose to turn on or off; they're just there. A smile, however, can be pasted over a mood to keep others from asking uncomfortable questions like "Hey, what's the matter?" This youngster also figures that no one really wants to hear his troubles anyway. This "he looks okay to me" belief is what often prevents parents from seeking help with an oppositional and defiant son or daughter until the problem has worsened.

Perspective #4: "Never, but never, let down your guard." Some youngsters believe that others are going to try to trick them into exposing their hurts and concerns. They might be fearful to discuss feelings, so they work hard at *not* having them. Because of their aggravation toward Mom, Dad, teacher, and other adults, these youngsters avoid honesty, fearing that awful things will happen if they ever discuss what's *really* bothering them (Chapter Six).

It is important to consider again that these perspectives are just that—ways of perceiving reality. They represent a view of what is going on, not necessarily what actually exists. Fortunately, changes to each of these perspectives can be influenced.

Influencing Changes

Note here that we are talking about *influencing* changes in the perspectives, not changing the perspectives directly. This is an important point because we (parents, teachers, and counselors) cannot directly change any perspective or attitude held by the child. They must change it themselves. We are empowered, however, to *influence* this change.

A Challenge. There's an old folktale that explains this idea perfectly. One winter the Sun and the Wind were observing an old man walking along the road. He was wearing a heavy coat. The Sun and the Wind made a wager regarding which one of them had the power and force to remove the old-timer's coat.

The bet was on; the Wind went first. He blew up a blustery gale, and blasted it squarely at the poor fellow, attempting to remove the coat by the sheer force of his gusts. But the Wind only caused the old man to cling even more tightly to the coat.

The Sun was next, only he took a totally different approach to the challenge. He spread his warming rays over the old man and patiently waited. It wasn't long before the man took off the heavy coat and carried it all the way home.

Keys to Change. Instead of a coat, the oppositional and defiant youngster is wearing his or her perspectives. Force directed at changing them only makes them more hardened and resistant to change. The only way to change any perspective is to change the reality, just as the Sun caused the old man to remove the heavy coat by warming the air around him.

Here are some suggestions for "warming the air" around each of the four perspectives when they are held by oppositional and defiant youngsters. Keep in mind also that, just as perspectives are not developed overnight, they do take a bit of time to change.

1. Unconditional positive regard. For youngsters who feel that they are affirmed only for what they do, a parent can begin by making affirmations unconditional. Years ago, psychologist Dr. Carl Rogers discussed what he called "unconditional positive regard," which he defined as praise, attention, and affirmation for "being" as opposed to "doing."

This can be a tough assignment for parents who haven't had much experience in regarding their children unconditionally. It's an assignment that is complicated even further by the fact that we live in a society where just about everything is brutally conditional and performance-based.

Consider complimenting your son or daughter on the fact that they bring you pleasure as you watch them grow and develop. Let them know that you appreciate their smile and their easy manner. Pay them sincere compliments when they are helpful to others, or when they demonstrate character, integrity, and honesty (even though some of this is performance-based, it does emphasize attributes that are attainable by anyone). Inform them that you are proud of them and their accomplishments, but mostly you are proud of them. Make them secure in the fact that you are going to find more "being" things than "doing" things to focus on in your relationship with them.

(Note: These suggestions are not intended to replace performance-based affirmations entirely. Where would our society be if everyone felt unconditionally regarded, but never *did* anything? The idea here is one of balance.)

2. *Sometimes it's "good enough."* Let your son or daughter know that "good enough" is sometimes good enough. Life is too short to fret over being able to do everything to absolute perfection. Besides, such fascination with perfection can stifle creativity. Research has shown time and time again that the most successful young adults were not those who had straight "A's" in school, but rather those who had a range of interests.

In the university I learned early on that I could put four hours of work into a project and get a "B+" or even an "A-" on it. I could spend ten to twenty hours on it and push the grade up to an "A." The role of husband and father collided sufficiently with my role as student that I opted for the

- 115 -

four-hour project many times. For me it wasn't an issue of being lazy as much as it was an issue of being practical.

I had the opportunity to try this "good enough" thing out on my son when he became a senior in high school. He was told that he had to take a class in calculus. Having never had that sort of math in any of my schooling, I wasn't much help to him, but I did know that all he needed to do was just pass the class to make it out of high school. That must have calmed his mind a bit, because his concerns eased up considerably—so much that he actually ended up with a "B" in the class.

Remember, we and our kids are in this thing for the long haul, and sometimes "good enough" really is good enough.

3. Suffering is permitted. Validate to your children that suffering is permitted. Better yet, model it. Now, we're not talking about a sick kind of nonstop suffering (that's reserved for folks who feel alive only when they can drain every drop of sympathy from those around them), but more of an honesty regarding unhappiness. If youngsters are afraid to recognize that they are unhappy because they fear the questions that might follow, you as the parent might try wording it in this fashion:

> *"You know, you really seem sort of down today. I'd really like to know if you are or not; and I promise I won't ask any more questions about it unless you bring it up."*

4. Let the guard down sometimes. Demonstrate to your youngster that there are times and situations when it is appropriate to let your guard down. Like Luke's parents in Chapter Seven, we can grow immensely in the eyes of our children when we expose our own vulnerability in the right set of circumstances. Luke came around quickly because he realized that not only were his folks able to accept some of the responsibility for the deterioration in their relationship, but they were fully willing to do it for Luke's sake. They successfully communicated to the boy that their relationship with him was much more important than their aggravation at his behavior. It worked, and it opened the door for him to express his own vulnerability. The result was authentic healing.

Sometimes issues tied to vulnerability and trust are still pretty raw for the child and not easily opened for discussion. It's then we might say, "I care about you, but I also care enough about you not to pry if it makes you uncomfortable." Back off for then, but rest assured that you have probably made it easier for the next time.

If My Kid's So Nice ... Why's He Driving ME Crazy?

Chapter Twelve

Fair, Reasonable, and a Little Fun

In the more than twenty years that I have been working with oppositional and defiant youngsters and the adults in their lives, it has been my observation that some of these adults always seem to be able to dodge the barbs and step over and around the traps that these youngsters set for them. They seem bulletproof to the effects of oppositional and defiant behavior.

If the oppositional and defiant youngster in your life happens to be in junior high or high school, it's likely that you have seen a few of these adults at the school. The kid has six different teachers throughout the day, and during conferences with each of them, you'll hear about three different opinions. One or two are apt to say that they hate to get up on Monday mornings knowing that in less than five minutes your son or daughter will ruin the rest of their week. Then there will be one or two who will say that they have some difficulty with your youngster in class, but no more than with the others. Finally, there will be one or two who will say that they get along well with your kid and wouldn't mind having a class full of students just like him or her.

Adults who can get along well with the oppositional and defiant youngster possess and demonstrate the ability to be fair and reasonable. But more importantly, they have the ability to make that fairness and reasonableness appear as such to the youngster (remember, improvement has little to do with reality and *everything* to do with the youngster's perspective). Also, they know how to have a little fun with the youngster. Let's look at these qualities separately.

Fairness

It's difficult for someone to become upset with an individual who is obviously trying to be fair. Fair dealing simply slices the anger right out of the picture. This is why folks in customer service say, "How can we make it right?" when confronted by an irate customer. It's difficult indeed to pick a fight with someone who won't fight.

Probably without realizing it, Luke's parents (Chapter Seven) were successful in communicating with their son because they were fair. Making it clear that the blame was not all Luke's, the father stated that if he needed to change, he was willing to do so. Luke believed his dad, not so much because of what he said to Luke that night, but because Luke knew his father's track record for being fair— something that had always been there.

I worked with one girl who felt that her teacher was deliberately trying to fail her. "She said that I have a lot of zeros because of missing homework, but I turned it in," the girl insisted. The teacher was pretty certain that the girl had *not* turned the work in, but avoided an argument by being fair about the whole thing. The teacher simply pulled the girl aside and made an appointment to meet with her. She shared that she was more than willing to change the grade if the girl could account for the missing work. She asked the student to bring in her assignment folder for that class.

When they met, the teacher calmly and softly shared that she would be happy to remove a zero in her grade book if the girl could show her a specific completed assignment for a lesson covered during a particular week (this teacher also made it a practice of returning work to the students after she recorded the grades). The teacher even went over the lessons and the assignments again so that the girl would recall them, all the while stating that she would *really* like to remove the zeros. The girl went through her folder and, of course, could not account for the missing work. She had no one else to blame at this point; she was out of excuses. The remaining zeros were also investigated in this fashion.

In this situation, the teacher demonstrated something I call "spontaneous mercy." She was fair enough to offer substantial credit for the missing work if the girl still *wanted* to do it. This act removed the fight from the girl and replaced it with responsibility. As I recall, she did do enough of the work to pass the class. Although the fairness that the teacher demonstrated did not cure all of this youngster's oppositional and defiant behavior, the girl stopped complaining about *that* teacher, and she did perform better in *that* class.

Fairness can often earn considerable dividends and reduce the level of grief for the adult involved.

Reasonableness

Folks who make a life's work of studying human character put reasonableness near the top of the list of positive human attributes. Like the person who is fair, an individual who is reasonable will experience little difficulty with others. Reasonableness has a way of removing the fuel from the fires of conflict.

Sometimes reasonableness is associated closely with fairness. Luke's folks were fair in assuming part of the blame for their conflict with the boy, but they were also reasonable, especially in the way they voiced their own vulnerability in the relationship.

Other times, reasonableness creates an impression that makes so much sense, it discourages disagreement. It is simply part of a good bargain.

For example, more than once I have had frustrated parents walk into my counseling office *without* their son or daughter. "He's sitting out in the car," they say to me. "He says he's not *ever* coming in here, and no one can make him. Listen, we've begged, pleaded, and even threatened. It's just no use."

At some point in the session I walk out to the car, stick my hand through the window (it always works best when the window is open!), and introduce myself. I have never— repeat, *never*—had a youngster refuse the gesture. Why? Because a kid would have to look like a 14-karat jerk to refuse the handshake of an agreeable, polite, well-intending stranger who is trying to help.

"You know, Robert," I begin, "I'm gonna take a guess and say that you're pretty upset with your folks right now. Am I right or wrong?" (Brilliant, huh?)

"Uh . . . you're right, I guess."

"Are you upset because you feel deceived or tricked or somehow forced to come here?" This is a pretty obvious question, I suppose, but a good one.

"A little of both." I can see him relax a bit.

"Can I sit in the car with you?" I ask. "I feel kinda silly just standing here." He nods, and I slip into the driver's seat.

"Robert, I'm going to ask you a question, and I want you to know that you don't have to answer it if you don't want to. Understand?" Again a nod.

"Is there more to it than being upset about coming to my office?" There is a prolonged silence before he speaks.

"Yeah . . . there's a lot more to it than that."

"I believe you. Thanks, that helps me understand things a little better." I carefully select my next words.

"I'm not in the miracle business, Robert," I continue, "but I think that I can help make things easier on you, and help your folks too. But you know what? It's going to be kinda hard to do it from the front seat of a Chevy." He grins a little. "Will you come in with me, and let me see what I can do?"

I have yet to be refused. Reasonableness works.

And a Little Fun

For parents and children in ongoing conflict, fun is all but lost. This is a shame, because humor and fun contain the very essence of healing. Laughter *is* great medicine.

My wife Bobbie is the most fun-loving person I know. She is thoroughly committed to trying just about anything once—twice if it doesn't kill her. I have seen her rappel down mountains, do loop-the-loops in gliders, and all kinds of stuff that I was too chicken to even consider. As a result, she has never lost the emotional resilience and sense of wonder of a young child.

Humor is where you find it—even in church. During a service I sat behind a mother and her young son. He was restless and being difficult. He wanted to stand during the sit-down parts of the service and sit during the stand-up parts. He sat down as we all stood for the prayer, and the mother abruptly yanked him to his feet. He studied his mother's face to make certain that her eyes were closed, then he quietly sat down during the prayer. Just as the "Amen" was being said, he quietly rose to his feet so that his mother would see him standing when she opened her eyes. Of course, when I shared this story with my wife (she was the boy's Sunday School teacher), she asked me how I was able to see all of this if *my* eyes had been closed. Ah, the price of research.

Humor can redirect. A good friend of mine was once an administrator of a residential treatment center for adolescent girls. One day a girl was cussing him out because he did not allow their unit to go to a carnival in a very rough part of town.

Halfway through her "blast" his eyes became enormous, and the expression on his face became one of exaggerated disbelief. She immediately became silent when he pointed to his sleeve.

"You spit on my shirt!" he exclaimed. She stammered, then paused, then laughed. She threw up her arms and walked away. The incident was over.

Spontaneity is a great source of fun, and when done in good faith, it almost always improves relationships. Food fights and water-gun duels are messy, but loads of fun. No harm is intended or taken, and everyone joins in on the cleanup.

In my counseling office I have a large Nerf ball. On occasion, I'll pop youngsters right between the eyes with it, partly to loosen them up a bit (the kids, not their eyes), and partly to observe their response. Usually the child grins, looks for the ball, then tosses it back at me. The message here is, "Life doesn't have to be so serious *all* of the time."

Unfortunately, families in conflict haven't had any real fun in a long, long time. For this reason, a little bit of fun is a good place to begin.

Chapter Thirteen

Reduce and Raise

With the oppositional and defiant youngster, the direct approach just doesn't work. When given instructions that work well with most youngsters, this kid finds creative ways to mess 'em up—and does it with amazing predictability. In fact, it is this predictability that inflicts so much pain and frustration. As we have seen, our most typical and gut-level responses to this youngster's behaviors have a way of backfiring on us. It's sort of like throwing a boomerang that's guaranteed to seek out and destroy the thrower!

Fortunately, whenever a parent begins to pull away from the struggles in a deliberate and planned fashion, the results can have a dramatic effect upon the behaviors that follow. If we remove the fuel, the youngster has more difficulty generating heat. (Note: There will be those times when a parent may choose to deliberately *add* some fuel as a part of a planned intervention. This will be covered in Chapter Fifteen.)

The most effective ways of minimizing struggles come through a simple formula that I call "*Reduce* and *Raise*."

This "formula," shown in Figure 13-1, involves reducing excessive expectations, overdependency, conditions, and rigidity, and raising the conscious awareness of the behavior. We will examine each of these in detail.

Reduce

expectations, overdependency, conditions, and rigidity

Raise

conscious awareness of behavior

The
"Reduce and Raise"
Formula

Figure 13-1

Reduce

The *Reduce* part of the formula addresses how the relationship between a parent and child (or between the child and other authority figures) can dramatically improve when we remove negative elements from it.

Excessive Expectations. The problem of excessive or unreasonable expectations, the sort that infest the parent-child relationship, was discussed in depth in Chapter Eight. When these expectations are reduced to the essentials that really matter, the change can be significant. Behaviors involving power struggles will lessen in just about every instance. It's not a total solution to the problem, but it's not a bad start.

Overdependency. Closely associated with excessive expectations is "overdependency," a term borrowed from the mental health profession. It is a condition that is imposed upon the child by the adult. In explaining overdependency in workshops and conferences, I like to use the following demonstration. I hold up a pen in each hand and explain that we are all born with a potential to function wholly and well. That potential is represented by two parts: left-hand pen and right-hand pen. Both are needed for a person to be whole, capable, and effective as a human being.

Then I ask for a female volunteer and equip her with a pen for each hand also. "As we begin to search for a life's mate to eventually marry, we do a very interesting thing," I comment. "We each exchange one pen." The volunteer and I demonstrate this for the audience.

"Assuming that we are about equal in our backgrounds, values, plans, and dreams, what does either of us gain or lose in this exchange, in terms of the grand scheme of things?" I ask. Of course the answer is that such an exchange should work out to a draw, with neither partner gaining or losing any substantial ground in the process. Most marriages are hopefully of this sort of exchange, or else someone is bound to be unhappy eventually.

Then I change the scenario and have the volunteer represent my adolescent daughter instead of my wife. As her father, I have some concerns about the way that she is "ruining her life." As a frustrated and frightened father, I might say:

"I can't believe how reckless you are. You are going to ruin your whole life long before you have an opportunity to make a good swap with an appropriate young man down the road. You're heading for disaster, that's what. I won't let that happen. Here, let me just keep one of these until you are better able to take care of it yourself."

I take one of the volunteer's pens. She now has one; I have three. This is overdependency. She is overdependent upon me to give something back to her. And I am in command of the terms.

This act on my part (representing the parent) creates immediate difficulties. She is not able to function as well.

She becomes frustrated, angry, and very resentful. Any and all mistakes that she makes are blamed on me, the parent. The father-daughter relationship takes a huge hit, and communication shuts down to zero. (Isn't it interesting to note that, as insensitive and unfair as I might be toward her, I am certainly *not* indifferent?) Instead of my action motivating her to improve, it has caused her to become even more troubled and ineffective. She will make it very clear in her behavior that she does not appreciate what I have done. But interestingly enough, there is usually a limit to just how much she will challenge me directly. In understanding the reason why, you will arrive at the very core of the internal workings of the oppositional and defiant youngster. She fears additional rejection, so the issue is not open to discussion. All of her "discussing" is done with behavior.

A counselor I once supervised had a case that centered around this issue of overdependency. This case was very briefly mentioned during the discussion of No-lution #6 in Chapter Five. A father referred his daughter. They were having fits. His biggest complaint was that she had an "attitude," and that she was failing the ninth grade of high school—for the third time! This added to the strain in their relationship, which the girl felt was essentially nonexistent anyway (due, of course, to her father's overcontrolling nature).

Near April of her first year in the ninth grade, Pop was concerned about her grades and asked her to "just pass!" She failed. About the same time of year the *second* time through the grade, her father again became fearful of her failing and begged her to "please, please, just pass!" She failed again.

Again it was the same time of the year, now the *third* time through the ninth grade. She was failing. The father became absolutely hysterical, pleading with her, "Just pass, please, please, just pass!" She failed again, of course. What interested me about this case was the fact that at no time did the girl ever discuss with her father the resentment she had toward him. Instead, she used her *behavior* to deliver the message.

This young lady was willing to sabotage at least three years of her *own* life in order to deliver her "message." If such a story doesn't grab your attention as to how stubborn and persistent oppositional and defiant behavior can be, not much of anything will.

The reduction of overdependency involves the giving back of what was taken away. This is much easier *said* than done, however, because the adults usually fear *horrible* consequences if they ever give up control. Parents feel that, without their intervention, the child's whole life will fall apart.

Conditions on the Relationship. The concept of conditional versus unconditional relationships between parents and their children has been discussed in previous chapters. Whereas expectations are spoken ("You'd *better* make the "A-B" Honor Roll this six weeks!"), conditions usually are not. In Chapter Eleven, "I am affirmed only for what I do" is the perspective youngsters have, reflecting a very powerful (and common) condition for getting the attention and approval of their parents.

In reducing the conditions attached to acceptance, nurturance, and affirmation (see the suggestions in Chapter

Eleven), a parent (or a teacher, in the case of the classroom environment) enhances unconditional positive regard—the very best kind.

Rigidity. Parental rigidity limits a youngster's decision-making skills. A "take it or leave it" or "it's my way or the highway" parental stance can not only poison the relationship, it can severely limit the child's sense of empowerment. The compulsive home, racked by drug abuse, alcoholism, or other compulsive disorders and behaviors, is usually quite rigid.

Not everything is negotiable, of course, but the practice of making choices available is of so much help in re-empowering the oppositional and defiant child, that we will devote the entire next chapter to it.

Raise

The *Raise* part of the formula addresses awareness. It takes a look "under the table" (Chapter Six), the place where oppositional and defiant behaviors begin. By helping youngsters to consider the connection between their behavior and the emotions that they prefer to keep hidden, real change can have a start.

In a sense, this is but a spin-off of the old "reverse psychology" idea that's been around since water, the "tell 'em what you think they are going to do so they'll decide they no longer want to do it" concept. An example might be: "Mary, be ready to go with us to the Smiths' house at 7:00 p.m. for dinner. Last time you were late. And I'm willing to bet anything that you're going to be late again. I'm probably right, huh?"

Although this approach does have its merit, it can be overused to the point of ineffectiveness. A better approach might be one like this:

> *"Johnny, I was kind of wondering if you were going to forget to put the trash out on the street like last week and the week before. I noticed that you 'forgot' to do it two times in a row now, and I'm wondering if you are trying to tell me something. I'm going to watch and see if you put the trash out this morning. If it doesn't get put out, maybe we need to discuss it tonight. What would be a good time for you?"*

This second approach certainly raises the awareness of trash-neglecting behavior, but it also considers that there might be a connection between the behavior *and* the relationship. Also, by suggesting *prior* to the chore that there might be a discussion required if the chore is not done, there's an excellent likelihood that the trash will get put out. I call this approach "Spit in the Soup," since it is a provocative sort of act. It directly calls attention to the behavior (noncompliance in this case) and addresses the possible reasons for it. It exposes the motive *and* the intent of the behavior that immediately follows.

The *Raise* part of the formula also addresses the predictability of the behavior. This youngster does not want to be predictable, and does not believe that he *is* predictable. "Spitting in this kid's soup" (with care not to inflame) can be a very expedient and direct way of getting to the issues behind the behaviors. This will be the topic of Chapter Fifteen.

Healthy Detachment

The parental reduction of excessive expectations, overdependency, conditional regard, and rigidity, coupled with strategic bouts of "spitting in this kid's soup," requires generous amounts of detachment. Healthy and appropriate detachment from our children is absolutely necessary at some point; but it is painful. In his eye-opening book *A World Waiting to Be Born*, M. Scott Peck says, "It is not the task of children to cooperate; it is their task to grow" (Peck, 1993). Peck reaffirms to me that conflicts are a component of *healthy* parent-child relationships. They're part of growing up. Through the gradual process of healthy detachment—the deliberate act of reducing the hold they have on their child—parents take a giant step toward more growth themselves.

As I said, detachment is painful for a parent. And it usually comes during one critical incident. For me it was the time my son Jamie told me that he was going to drive from southern Texas to Montreal and back—by himself. I asked him in no uncertain words to reconsider. Canada was a long way off, not a venture for someone alone. I could have insisted that he not go, but he was twenty years old. He didn't *need* my permission; I let him go. It was painful watching him drive off and not being certain that I would ever see him again. It hurt like crazy, but I let him go.

It was several days before I heard from him. In the meantime I had trouble sleeping, imagining all that could happen to a young man alone on such a trip (this was not long after Michael Jordan's father was murdered as he was traveling alone). I finally had to come to the realization that, whatever happened, I had been 100% appropriate as a father in this matter. If he ended up broke, stranded, sick, or dead, I would just have to deal with it. I prayed for his safety and my sanity; then I let it go. I slept after that.

Chapter Fourteen

Choices

The act of offering a youngster choices paves the way to changed behavior. It does more than just break down rigidity and reduce conditions, excessive expectations, and overdependency (thus operating from the *Reduce* side of the *Reduce* and *Raise* Formula); it empowers. When choices are available, decisions are possible. Decision-making empowers, and empowerment makes change possible. It's that simple.

When I was in high school, there was a rule: no student could chew gum in class. In fact, having a stick of gum in your pocket back then would be roughly equivalent to carrying a pistol to class today. You only had to examine the bottoms of the school desks at the end of May to figure out how well this rule was followed. One of my teachers, a Korean Conflict veteran, was wise enough in the ways of freshmen to know that coming down too hard on the gum thing would end up making him more of a policeman ("I know there's gum in your mouth, so open up and let me take a look") than a teacher. Besides, I knew one kid who could cheek a wad of bubble gum so well that the FBI would never find it.

This teacher did a truly brilliant thing. He allowed us a minute or two to either put our gum in the trash can, swallow it whole, or put it on a piece of paper to be retrieved and re-chewed (yum!) later at a more appropriate time. The choice was ours; the struggle was over.

Two Considerations

First of all, this chapter is not meant to imply that *everything* is open to choice. In certain ways, our children probably have too many choices already. Sometimes a hard stand on an issue is the best thing, especially when safety is involved. If a mother discovers that her three-year-old is playing with a rattlesnake in the back yard, she doesn't give the child the option of putting the snake down now or in five minutes. And families who hold to values of honesty, truth, and morality don't open these virtues to negotiation (although it seems to me that other elements in our environment do it all the time).

The second consideration is so obvious that it is easily overlooked. Even when a parent is extremely rigid, thereby removing all choice from the table, there is always at least one powerful choice remaining—the choice to defy. Whenever it seems that there are no choices left, the choice to defy *always* remains. So, if we are going to offer choices one way or the other, doesn't it just make good sense to offer the sort of choices that will bring compliance, reduce aggravation, and leave relationships intact?

Parents can offer their child six different categories of choices: involvement, task, time, activity, reward, and consequence (these are listed in Figure 14-1, along with an added seventh category that we will call "turbocharged"). As we look at these, consider how they might work with your son or daughter. We'll also consider how to make the choices appear even more attractive to the youngster.

Types of Choices

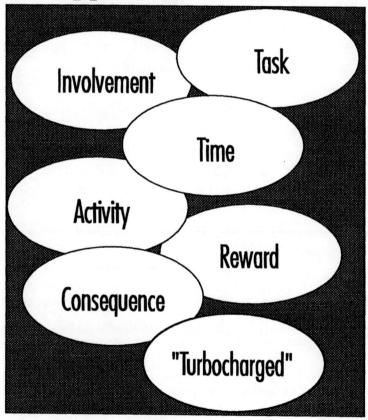

Figure 14-1

Choice of Involvement

Especially with adolescents, there comes a point where parents realize that they can't physically force the youngster to *do* much of anything. Never did I realize this to be the case more than when I conducted psychological assessments with juveniles who were going up on charges to federal court. As if telling one of these kids "Now you just sit down here and cooperate with me or I'll tell the judge" would really make him put on the brakes. What did he have to lose? He was already in detention.

What worked, and worked well, was a careful and straightforward explanation of the truth:

> *"Johnny, I'm supposed to do some testing with you. The judge has ordered it. I'm going to tell you right now that you don't have to do any of it—not a bit. I'll write a short report to the judge saying that you didn't want to do it, and that'll be the end of my part of it. At that point, whatever happens is between you and the judge. If you decide that you want to work with me on this, I'll write in my report that you were cooperative. It could help you in court. If you'd like, I'll give you some time to think it over."*

Did you notice the reasonableness here (Chapter Twelve)? Over a period of four years I did a few hundred of these assessments. Using this strategy, I *never* had a youngster refuse. I'm proud of that.

Depending on the age and maturity of the youngster, alternatives to involvement can be offered. If you are asking a child to join you and the rest of the family for dinner at a friend's house, choices might include "We could drop you off at Grandma's, and you could do your homework there while we go to dinner," or "The Martins said you could bring a friend if you like," or "We could call and ask Becky (the sitter) to come over while we're gone." Of course it's alright to add a little incentive ("The Martins said we'll be having grilled hamburgers and homemade peach ice cream before we go down to the lake to watch the fireworks"). The secret to the effectiveness of these choices is that they must be attractive to the child and reasonable to the adult.

Choice of Task

Because a youngster really isn't offered a choice of whether to do homework or not, tasks (and hassles) at home generally involve the completion of chores. Given a list of two or three chores to do, the oppositional and defiant youngster is apt to spend more time *complaining* about the tasks than *doing* them.

An excellent way to handle this problem is to write the chores down on cards, one per card (draw pictures of the chores for children who are too young to read), then hand the youngster five or so cards of the chores that need to be done. Tell him that if he is willing to get started right away, he would only need to do three of them—he can give two cards back, and not have to do those two chores. What a deal! Although no intervention works perfectly all of the time, it's tough for the child to whip up an argument for this one. It is reasonable, and it again empowers the youngster to make a decision to *do* the chores rather than *punish* the parent.

If you are assigning chores to more than one youngster, make up enough cards to be distributed evenly. Spread them out face up on a table. Come up with some way for a youngster to go first (flip a coin, guess a number, draw straws, or whatever), then allow each child to take a turn selecting a chore card until they are all gone.

For the youngster who wants to complain when he is given even one chore, tell him that you have a chore for him on your list, but that he can pass on it. Inform him that he *must*, however, take the second one on the list. What he quickly finds out is that the second chore is always more involved, difficult, and time-consuming than the first. Hopefully, he learns to accept the initial chore with less complaining and arguing.

Choice of Time

Bedtime. Let's say that lights-out bedtime for a youngster is 9:00 p.m. during a school week. Although that time is not negotiable, all of the time leading up to it is. What difference would it make to you as a parent if Suzie played quietly in her room from 8:30 to 8:50 p.m., then prepared for bed (bath, brushing teeth, pajamas, etc.), or if she prepared for bed from 8:30 to 8:40 p.m., *then* played quietly in her room until lights out? Either option accomplishes the same end at 9:00 p.m., so it should make little or no difference to the adult. The freedom and opportunity to have the choice, however, can make *all* the difference to the child—with considerably less grief involved.

Chores. It is expected that the youngster will complete a few chores at home, but giving a time frame for their completion might just remove the struggle and the need for constant reminders. If three chores are to be completed, with each taking about five minutes, try giving the child an hour to complete all three of them. She can do all of them at once, then enjoy the remainder of the free time; or she can space them out with free time in between; or she can have the free time first, then finish the chores last. This bargain amounts to giving the child the choice, then holding her to the agreement that, whichever way she chooses to handle the chores, they will be completed by the end of the hour. This intervention also teaches the child a few basics of time management.

Homework. Even with homework, some choice is possible. When and where homework is to be done might be negotiable. For instance, is it to be done before dinner or after dinner, and can it be done in the living room, kitchen, den, or bedroom?

You might want to try a "bedtime bonus" if your child is having trouble collecting and completing homework. I came upon this idea when my son was having difficulty in the seventh grade. He had a homework list, which was to be checked off by each teacher and a parent, but he was having great difficulty getting the teacher's initials on the list after each class because of the crowd (the students would gather around the teacher immediately after the bell).

"Well, which is more important to you, Dad," he would exclaim to me, "to get their initials, or to be on time for my next class?"

See the trap here? Pretty sharp maneuvering on his part, and it had me stumped before I figured out a way around it. I decided to make no issue of a complete set of teacher initials; instead, I offered him an incentive of staying up fifteen minutes later at bedtime on any day that he had collected all of the initials without being tardy.

The plan worked like a charm until the day he missed a teacher's initials. He begged and he pleaded to stay up later. I calmly explained that he was not being punished; he would just be going to bed at the *regular* time. As I recall, there were no other arguments about the initials.

Choice of Activity

Most of the time family recreation and activities are somewhat flexible. Providing the youngster an occasional opportunity to plan a family activity or outing not only teaches the youngster valuable skills of organization, it empowers the youngster to accomplish a specific task in an agreeable manner. As an additional benefit, the child will probably be more cooperative while engaged in an activity that he or she created.

This can be a very effective intervention, and the grief saved can certainly be your own. A few years back I did some consulting with a residential facility for girls. One ongoing problem surfaced every time the staff tried to get the girls loaded into the van to go out on a staff-planned activity (such as going swimming, or to the zoo or mall, or out to eat). A third of the girls wanted to go, a third wanted to do something else, and a third just wanted to remain comatose in front of the TV. By simply having each girl plan an activity on a rotating basis, the griping and complaining all but disappeared. Every girl knew that if she complained too much, she'd catch the same whenever it was her turn. It taught them all to be a little more considerate of each other. It was also interesting to note that after this plan went into effect, the relationship between the girls and the staff improved.

This intervention requires some preparation and direction on the part of a parent. The child needs to be aware of issues and circumstances that will affect the activity—things like time, distance, budget, and other resources (help from adults would be an example of a resource). You should give them the tools, but you don't have to give them the world!

It would benefit this youngster if every family member made it a point, in some way, to recognize the child's efforts at putting together the activity. Following the activity, notes could be posted on the refrigerator or on the "Important Things to Remember" Board. As yet another thought, a thank-you card, signed by all, could be mailed to the child or placed at his or her spot at the breakfast table. What an incentive for the youngster to do even better next time!

Choice of Reward

The homework checklist plan worked because, for a period of time, the oppositional and defiant youngster does best when a benefit for compliance is *added*, instead of something being removed for noncompliance. This is a very important point, especially when beginning some of these interventions. When things are continually removed, the youngster loses interest and can even become discouraged. Under these conditions anger continues to fester, a sure-fire deterrent to progress and healing. Ultimately, however, the youngster will realize that the world is not going to go around handing him medals for doing what he is *expected* to do (but wouldn't it be fantastic if state troopers only pulled over the best drivers, praised their driving habits, and gave them restaurant gift certificates?). I *am* saying that recognizing compliance is a way to initially keep it going. In addition to recognizing and rewarding compliance, try offering choices in the type of recognition or reward received.

I worked with one special education teacher who had a marvelous system in place for the recognition of effort and compliance. I was standing in the hall one day when I heard her tell one student that he had earned either free time on the computer or a garbage pull. The words "garbage pull" grabbed my attention, so I peeked. She had a small, grey, "Oscar the Grouch"-type trash can on the corner of her desk. Inside were all kinds of goodies, including games, candy, and a few school supplies. The kid chose the garbage pull, which meant that he had to put one hand over his eyes and reach in and pick out a prize with the other. It worked well, especially considering that this was a classroom full of very emotionally and behaviorally disordered youngsters.

A refinement of this idea would be to write down a number of different kinds of rewards—ranging, say, from extra TV time to lunch at McDonald's. Put each reward in a separate envelope, then let the youngster do an "envelope pull." So that sincere verbal praise is not overlooked, let the contents of at least one of the envelopes read, "A parent's expression of sincere appreciation for a job well done." Don't be surprised if this one becomes their favorite. Kids still love to hear it.

Choice of Consequence

This intervention resembles rewards, only it's in reverse. Its most significant advantage lies in the fact that the child *participates* in the selection of the consequence for the violation of a rule. For this intervention to work effectively, it is critical that the most important family rules be made clear to everyone. Next, several different, but appropriate, consequences for violating each rule are brainstormed by the whole family. These consequences might include reduction of weekly allowance, writing lines, earlier bedtime, or a cutback in TV time. The more consequences that can be generated, the better.

As a symbol of agreement, each consequence is initialed by every family member, then it is placed into an envelope. The envelopes then are grouped with rubber bands according to the rule they address. Whenever there is a violation, the youngster is asked to draw an envelope and accept the consequence inside.

The youngster can't complain that the consequences are excessive, or even that you made them up on the spot out of anger at him or her. Everyone, including the youngster, has already agreed upon the consequences from the beginning (an important consideration that takes advantage of the fact that the youngster can be much more rational *before* there is trouble than after).

I knew of one nine-year-old who worked himself into a pretty tough jam. He lived in a group home, a cottage-type environment with other youngsters and a set of houseparents. Since most of these boys had been abused before coming to the group home, corporal punishment (spanking) was not an option. For instance, as a consequence for lying, these youngsters, and the children in the other cottages as well, wrote lines, such as "Lying is wrong, and it only creates more trouble."

This boy was given a consequence by his housepop to write two hundred or so lines. The boy rebelled. The housepop increased the lines until they were somewhere around a thousand. The thousand lines so overwhelmed the boy that he couldn't get started, plus he was still plenty angry and didn't want to do them anyway. His problem was that he was supposed to have a home visit during the upcoming weekend, and his family told him, "No lines, no home visit." His output for a whole day spent on this task was exactly *one* line.

The houseparents were concerned. They didn't want to keep him from a home visit with his family, but neither did they want to back down on the consequence because important principles were at stake. They couldn't even change the consequence to something else (such as a chore) because the boy would use it as an opportunity to draw the houseparents and the other boys into a struggle. The lines *were* the best consequence, but a way was needed to get him started and keep him going until they were completed.

Cutting back the number of lines was considered, but it seemed like it would be giving in to the boy before he did *anything*. Besides, his one and only line spoke volumes about how stubborn he was determined to be (wasn't it interesting that he did write the single line, as if to prove that he wasn't *completely* unreasonable).

We came up with the envelope idea, with each envelope containing a bonus "deal" that would apply only to the amount of lines completed during a specified time period. In other words, the "deal" would require some *up-front* output on his part before he would even find out what the payoff was.

On several slips of paper the houseparents wrote, "This coupon makes the lines you wrote count one and a half times," or "This coupon makes the lines you wrote count double," or "This coupon makes the lines you wrote count triple." Each one of these was folded several times and sealed in its own envelope. The housepop approached the youngster with several envelopes and a timer and said:

> *"I have a way here to help you get started on this. Pick one of these envelopes and keep it where you can see it at all times. Make sure your eyes never leave the envelope, okay?"*

The child selected an envelope and put it on his desk next to his paper and pen. The housepop continued:

> *"The envelope has a special deal in it for you—a deal that depends upon how many lines you write before this timer goes off. Ready?"*

He set the timer and left the room (knowing this kid, the housepop probably took the timer with him to a place that was within earshot). The boy began writing, and when the timer went off, the housepop came back into the room.

The boy opened his envelope to discover that the lines he had written counted double. This approach worked; both of them were delighted. The youngster finished the lines in time to go on the family visit. But even if he hadn't done one single line while the timer was running, this little fellow would soon have realized that the housepop had gone out of his way to be fair and reasonable.

Please note that this arrangement is very different from *promising* to count lines double if the youngster would only get busy. That would be close to an outright bribe. In contrast, this youngster was required to initiate and *produce* something before the "deal" could apply. It's a different situation altogether.

"Turbocharged" Choices

What would happen if a mother gave her son or daughter five chore cards, asked the youngster to do three of them, then offered to do the remaining two chores herself? Would it affect the completion and the quality of the work of the child's chores? Sure it would. It would boost, or turbocharge, the very likelihood of the chore being done, and being done well.

What would happen if a father devised chore cards for three children to select from, only to have one card left, at which he exclaimed, "And I'll do this one!"? Wouldn't the kids know that the last card on the table would be the most distasteful and disgusting chore of all, something like cleaning all of the bathrooms in the house or bathing the cat (ugh!)? Would Dad's gesture make a point about being fair, reasonable, and a little fun (Chapter Twelve)? Of course it would.

If My Kid's So Nice ... Why's He Driving ME Crazy?

Chapter Fifteen

Spit in the Soup

Can You Imagine?

You are enjoying lunch with an old friend. Suddenly you lean over, and in full view of God and everybody, you spit right into your friend's bowl of potato soup. No question about it, unless your friend is no longer maintaining operational body temperature, you *will* get a response. Your friend might only look at you in disbelief, or ask you if you've lost your mind, or perhaps call for his or her check and leave in a huff. It's also possible that your friend just might spit back in *your* soup, prompting a food fight that would get the two of you tossed out of that restaurant with an admonition never to come back again.

In later explaining why you spit into your friend's soup, there are a number of excuses you could make. You could say that you did it because you were upset with your friend, or that your friend had been ignoring you, or even that you were curious to see what your friend would do. You could even apologize for it, and ask for your friend's forgiveness. One thing you could *not* do, however, is claim that your behavior was an accident. You would have a difficult time convincing anyone that your face just wandered too close to their soup bowl and at that exact instant the saliva jumped right out of your mouth! No, a behavior like that would be provocative—clearly done on purpose.

Go ahead. I <u>dare</u> you!

Raise

In attempting to deal with a child's oppositional and defiant behavior, provocative action on the part of the parent is sometimes called for. Obviously, provocative action operates on the *Raise* side of the *Reduce* and *Raise* Formula (Chapter Thirteen). It makes everyone acutely aware of the child's behaviors that follow. In essence, that provocative action draws the "first blood," so to speak, signaling to the youngster that you are expecting a conflict, and that you are prepared for it.

Why is this sort of intervention so effective? Simple— you are prepared for the conflict, but the youngster is not (never say never, of course; some youngsters are *always* prepared for conflict). You have drawn the battle lines, something which often saps the fight right out of the kid.

Why Johnny Won't Fight

He's afraid of being direct. This youngster is passive rather than aggressive in his behaviors against authority figures because he does not want a showdown (as discussed in Chapters Six and Thirteen). He fears that if there is a showdown, he will lose face, power, and affection. Caught in this predicament, the youngster is apt to comply.

A Word of Warning

Whenever you invite a conflict, you are playing with fire. Obviously, provocative behavior that is punitive or embarrassing to the youngster could make things much worse. Any behaviors toward the child or adolescent that contain sarcasm, or cause the youngster to question your approval or affection toward them, should always be avoided.

Make the Message Clear

There's a knack to making provocative behavior work for you as a parent. You want your action to throw the child into enough of a bind that he or she will have to think before responding.

Here's how you do it. Let this youngster be in charge of the "Important Things to Remember" Board for a week. The "Important Things to Remember" Board is the family's clearinghouse for all correspondence between everyone, adults and children alike. It is put in a prime location in the house (like on the refrigerator or bathroom mirror), and there is absolutely no excuse for anyone not checking it in the morning and in the afternoon. In fact, it might be helpful to have a place on the Board for family members to check off that they have read it (thus helping to ensure that dental appointments, cheerleader tryouts, and "I'll be home a bit later today because _____" messages will be heeded.

Whenever it is Johnny's or Joanie's turn to post the messages on the Board for the day or week, hand the youngster a message that reads like this:

Dear Johnny (or Joanie):

At 7:00 p.m. we are going over to the Smiths' house for dinner. The last time we went over there, you were twenty minutes late getting home, and we had to wait on you. It was not a pleasant evening for any of us. I was just wondering—should I worry

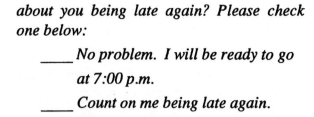

about you being late again? Please check one below:

_____ No problem. I will be ready to go

at 7:00 p.m.

_____ Count on me being late again.

Now is this a provocative statement or what? Notice that it doesn't threaten or excessively provoke (it *has* to provoke a little; that's the whole purpose). Either way, whichever statement the youngster checks, his or her behavior will be the focus of attention—and the kid knows it. If Johnny checks that he will be ready, a number of worn-out excuses have been eliminated (such as "Oh, I forgot!"). If he checks that he will be late again, you are now dealing with *openly* defiant behavior, where the issue is on top of the table and open to discussion.

Rarely would the youngster check that he or she *intends* to be late. Rather than doing that, Johnny or Joanie would probably leave both statements unchecked—a typical oppositional and defiant response. It doesn't matter, however, because if Johnny was in charge of the "Important Things to Remember" Board, he couldn't say that he didn't see the message. Any way he turns, he's responsible.

Getting to the Issues

The "Spit in the Soup"-type of intervention can also be used to encourage youngsters to discuss their behavior with you. The successful conclusion of Luke's story in Chapter

Seven points to the obvious benefits of doing this. Another word of caution, however: it must be handled very carefully.

Sit down with the youngster when it seems to be a good time for a discussion. Have several examples of her most recent oppositional and defiant behaviors in mind, and share these with her in a rather matter-of-fact manner. The advantage of having four or so examples is that it establishes the fact that you are serious in confronting these behaviors. And, although she might be inclined to offer excuses for one or two of the behaviors as isolated incidents, four is substantial enough to indicate a pattern of ongoing behavior. Hopefully, she'll just be quiet and listen.

Explain that it seems to you that she sometimes has difficulty doing what authority asks. If she has similar difficulties at school also (such as general irresponsibility regarding schoolwork), mention them. Then ask her if your observations make any sense to her at all. Rarely will a youngster respond with an emphatic "No." At this point, if you have done *your* homework well, you just might begin to communicate with this youngster at a more substantial level.

Restate your regard for her, just as Luke's father did with him (Chapter Seven). Share that you have concerns about how your relationship with her has been affected, then encourage her to share her feelings with you as openly as possible. Relate that you are certain that you are not the perfect parent and that, without meaning to, you might sometimes do or say things that make her angry or hurt her feelings. Share that you want to know about these things so that you can change them.

Do not judge or evaluate what she says. Thank her for taking the risk to be honest with you, and share that you will consider all that she has said, and that you will work on changing your own behavior so that things will improve. Then do it.

Cues and Signals

It is helpful to explain to the youngster that oppositional and defiant behaviors are often "automatic," done without much thought or preparation. To help youngsters become more aware of these behaviors, offer to give them a nonverbal cue or signal whenever one of these behaviors is happening. It might be a light squeeze on the shoulder, for instance, that says to the youngster, "This is one of those behaviors that we talked about." If the behavior persists, and it might, try whispering, "I just gave you a message; did you get it?" Either way, compliance or noncompliance after that point should be a ready topic for discussion later ("Say, do you remember when I touched you on the shoulder this afternoon . . . ?").

Don't Remind Me!

Sometimes youngsters agree to do something for you, then put it off seemingly all day. Whenever you remind them of the chore, they are likely to snap back at you, "You don't have to keep reminding me about it; I'll take care of it after I'm through _____" (you can fill in the blank with the behavior that aggravates you most).

(Dr. Russell Barkley [1987] suggests that many youngsters are noncompliant because every minute they can avoid doing what a parent wants them to do is one more minute that they can keep on doing what *they* want to do. Isn't it interesting to note that this same behavior also works in reverse, with parents putting off completing a task for a child?)

Try this. After the youngster agrees to do something for you, don't mention the actual chore again. After some time has gone by, if you're afraid the youngster might have forgotten, simply say, "You know, it really is great knowing that I don't have to keep bugging you and reminding you to do things that you said you will do—don't you agree." I call this the "No Reminder" Reminder.

Mower Madness

A few years back, when both of my children were still living at home, I asked my son to be certain to mow the grass sometime during the day. It was a Saturday, and he had his six-foot, four-inch frame sprawled out all over the den. He was seriously engaged in watching about twenty episodes of cartoons.

"No problem, Dad," he said without taking his eyes off the TV. "I'll take care of it."

I was gone most of the day, and returned to the house just before dusk. The grass had not been cut, but he must have heard me coming around the corner. He raced out of the front door, pulled the lawnmower out of the garage, gave the rope one tug, and then as I pulled into the drive, he threw his hands up in a gesture of "What do you expect me to do; the darned thing won't start."

Was I upset? Yup. Did he have all day to accomplish this simple task? Certainly. Did I feel like giving this kid a piece of my mind? Absolutely. Would it have gotten the lawn mowed? Probably not. Would it have started an argument that would have ruined what remained of the weekend? Most definitely.

I tried to keep all of these things in mind as I got out of the car and approached him and the lawnmower.

"Won't start?" I asked. He nodded. "Well, it's probably not getting any fire."

"Fire?" he questioned. "What are you talking about, Dad?"

"This thing right here," I returned, as I disconnected the ignition wire from the spark plug. "Hold this a minute, and we'll check it."

"How will I know it's getting fire?" he questioned.

"Oh, you'll know," I said, as I gave the rope a yank. He must have shot three whole feet off the ground.

"Fire ain't the problem, Dad!" he exclaimed.

So maybe I only imagined that part of it—no, I didn't *really* shock him (although the *thought* of it did provide some relief). I did, however, remove the spark plug. I cleaned it up a bit with my pocket knife, and told him that sometimes plugs get so fouled that the engine won't start. I replaced the plug, reconnected the ignition wire, and gave the rope no more than a couple of pulls (honest).

The mower started. There was nothing else for him to do except cut the grass.

I must admit that, on this occasion, I did the *right* thing. I didn't really want to fight that evening with one of three people that I love more than life itself. But I did want the yard mowed. Was the spark plug really fouled? I don't know—probably not—but I do know it was better to put the blame onto a small chunk of ceramic and steel than to put it on him.

In this case cleaning the plug was a provocative act because it left him with no excuse; it also resulted in the grass being cut.

SPCs

"SPC" stands for Strategically Placed Compliment. They are especially handy to use around oppositional and defiant children and adolescents.

See, here's the problem: On the one hand, if you don't compliment youngsters when they do a task well and in a timely fashion, they are apt to think that you either didn't notice or just don't care. On the other hand, these youngsters often have trouble with compliments. Sometimes a child will toss the compliment back at you, which can incite an argument.

But with an SPC, you pay the compliment, then immediately shift to asking an unrelated question. When you strategically place the compliment before a question, the child usually responds to the question and lets the compliment settle.

A few years back I was doing group counseling with some girls who lived together in a therapeutic group home (the facility eventually became the residential treatment center that I spoke of earlier). One girl—we'll call her Mary—began crying as she shared about an incident in her life. Tracie was sitting across from Mary, and responding to Mary's tears, she walked across the room to bring her friend a tissue. She patted Mary on the shoulder, then walked back to her seat.

I had a feeling that this little gesture was more for Tracie's sake than Mary's (a tissue often communicates "Dry it up, you're making me uncomfortable"; the ultimate solution, offer the *whole* box). But I did want to recognize the positive aspects of Tracie's gesture.

I had one problem, though. I knew that if I paid that compliment to Tracie, she would probably have shouted, "Well, someone had to do it; she bawls like that all the time!" That would have ruined the whole thing.

So I strategically placed the compliment. "Tracie, that was a sweet thing that you did for Mary," I said. "It really pleases me whenever I see you girls responding to the needs and feelings of one other." Then, before she could say a word, I injected, "By the way, girls, we're going out to eat next week. Where would you like to go?" Tracie never had a chance to spoil it.

Sweeten the Deal

Compliments are fine, but sometimes even more tangible recognition is called for. Here are several suggestions for rewarding the completion of tasks.

"Caught You!" Awards. If all of the youngsters in your house have a set time to complete chores, consider implementing the "Caught You!" Awards. These could be printed awards or coupons for items or privileges.

Set a timer to go off sometime during chores. Tell the children that, whenever the timer goes off, they will win an award *if* they are actually doing a chore during that instant. Not only does this approach make it more likely that chores will get done, it is fun to do. If you have a camera that creates an instant photograph, you can even take a picture of the youngsters and what they were doing when the timer went off. Put these photographs up on the "Important Things to Remember" Board.

If you happen to be creative, there are lots of ways to modify this strategy. You can even make it apply to different situations other than chores, and use it in combination with other strategies.

Slip and Draw. This one is a spin-off of other strategies. Every time youngsters complete a chore or a homework assignment, give them a slip of paper ("certify" the slips by putting your initials on one side with a colored pen), then ask them to sign the slip, fold it, and put it in a coffee can with a slit cut in the lid. At the end of several days or a week, simply have a drawing for a prize. To "sweeten" this deal, put the prize in a very conspicuous place, with a sign on it that says, "To be given away Saturday." Youngsters should figure out pretty quickly that the more slips they have in the can, the better chance they have of winning the prize. The more slips, the more completed tasks—*and* the fewer hassles.

The Magic Box. This one will be discussed again in the next chapter, but it is a great strategy worth noting here too. Build a small box with a hinged lid, then put several hasps and locks on the lid. Place a prize or reward in the box, close the lid, and lock all of the locks. Let the youngster know that he can have what is in the box as soon as he earns all of the keys that will unlock it. Upon the completion of a task, or a certain predetermined group of tasks, the child receives a key to one of the locks. When he earns the last key, he can open the box and have the prize inside.

This little strategy has a number of benefits, but one of the best ones is the self-perpetuating nature of earning keys and unlocking locks. The youngster gets to do his chores and have fun with the box too!

If My Kid's So Nice ... Why's He Driving ME Crazy?

Chapter Sixteen

School

Compliance a Must

Compliance at school is, without question, a high priority. If Junior never makes his bed he will not fail family, but if he does little or nothing in his studies, he certainly will fail the fourth grade.

The connection between the noncompliance of underachievement and oppositional and defiant behavior is not a new discovery. In 1969 a doctoral student named Morrison studied underachievement in a group of preadolescent boys. She found an unusually high rate of passive aggression in these youngsters ("passive aggression" is an old term for one type of oppositional and defiant behavior). Twelve years later another doctoral student named Sutton (sound familiar?) studied passive-aggressive features of what was then called Oppositional Disorder (Sutton, 1981). He discovered that youngsters who presented these behaviors tended to have significant school achievement problems. What is interesting about these two pieces of research is that they both came to the same conclusion—even though they arrived at it from somewhat different directions.

If the oppositional and defiant child were to sit down and carefully plan how to achieve the biggest bang for his behavioral buck, failure to achieve tasks at school would be the way to do it. He could then upset his teachers and pull his folks into the struggle as well. For at least three reasons, then, school becomes an excellent place to launch the strongest program of attack against this youngster's noncompliance, forgetting, misunderstanding, and other prime oppositional and defiant behaviors.

Reason #1: Noncompliance is costly. The ultimate cost of noncompliance is failure and retention in grade. It does seem strange to fail and retain a student who has done very well on achievement tests, but this is often the case (again we reference Dr. Morrison, 1969). Progress in school, however, is measured by what a student *does*, not what a student is *capable* of doing. Of course, there is the hope that failure and retention in grade just might be the thing to jolt this kid into a perpetual state of academic output. Yeah, right. Holding the youngster back in grade seems like a great idea—until it's *your* kid.

Reason #2: Compliance is being modeled. Compliance, task completion, and other positive behaviors are being modeled continuously. In any given school classroom, most students are doing exactly what is expected of them. The oppositional and defiant youngster doesn't have to look far to figure out what he or she is *supposed* to be doing.

Reason #3: Teachers can help. Teachers can assist the parents, and are better equipped to handle this youngster's aggravating behaviors. They have the advantage of broader knowledge of young people. And, because of their status as professionals and their experiences with many children over the years, teachers are not as apt to be emotionally provoked by this child.

The Ideal Parent-Teacher Conference

The parent-teacher conference needn't be a distasteful, hand-wringing experience. Attention to the following tips (summarized in Figure 16-1) will help to assure a pleasant and productive conference:

Tip #1: Take the initiative. Whether it's handling an overdue bill, coming in late to work, or having a conference with your child's teacher, it's always better if you take the initiative to address the problem. Even if it was the teacher or the administrator who called for the meeting, your taking the initiative in the discussion helps to send the school the message that you are aware of the problem, and that you are interested in working with the school to resolve it. It also gives you an element of control. In attending the conference, be punctual, positive, and personable.

Tip #2: Stick to the issues. The conference is not being held to discuss your competency as a parent any more than it is being held to discuss the teacher's competency as an educator. The issues involve the youngster and what can be done to improve his or her compliance at school, so stick to that. Don't be afraid to speak up; you will be respected for it. Besides, you will have better information than the teacher regarding the child's history of school behavior, as well as related problems of noncompliance at home.

Tip #3: Examine the facts. Exactly what are the concerns—completion of tasks, getting along with others, manipulation, procrastination, obstructionism, forgetting, stubbornness? Identify these. Does the child "specialize" in certain types of oppositional and defiant behavior? Do these behaviors occur persistently or only sporadically? Does the youngster have any noted strengths and assets? What about the child's basic personality and how he or she gets along with others?

Tip #4: Look at long-range outcomes. Is this child *only* frustrating you and the teacher, or is there a real danger of failure and grade retention? Are there any signs of anxiety and/or depression? If the child's behavior were to remain essentially unchanged, how might it influence or affect him or her as an adult? These are tough questions, but ones worth asking.

Tip #5: Develop a unified plan. Make a decision with the teacher about what will be done concerning the problems. Anticipate what the child's responses might be, then work out a plan for dealing with them also. If there is more than one educator present at this conference, or if your spouse attends the conference with you, make certain that every person has some part in the plan. Determine how each person will be accountable.

7 Tips

for a Parent-Teacher Conference

1. Take the initiative.
2. Stick to the issues.
3. Examine the facts.
4. Look at long-range outcomes.
5. Develop a unified plan.
6. Set the next meeting.
7. Send an acknowledgement.

Figure 16-1

Tip #6: Set the next meeting. It is always best to establish a date and time for the next conference. By doing so, the next meeting might well be a time for rejoicing, and not the focal point for more discomfort and embarrassment. This is a very important step that is often skipped. Don't skip it.

Tip #7: Send an acknowledgement. Teachers are only human; they like to know that they are appreciated. This simple step of sending a follow-up note to the teacher (and the principal also, if appropriate) will encourage him or her to work especially hard with your child.

The remaining sections of this chapter will discuss four main issues: placement options; strategies and interventions for accomplishing compliance at school; how to deal with homework; and approaches for achieving effective discipline with the oppositional and defiant youngster.

Placement Considerations

Occasionally noncompliance and oppositional and defiant behaviors are serious enough to warrant special placement of the youngster at school. The threat of failure with retention in grade is the most common reason for this action. Other reasons might involve other difficulties at school, such as learning disabilities, social problems, and concerns regarding the child's basic psychological and emotional functioning. Although there are a number of kinds of placements, the most popular one by far is the one referred to as Special Education.

Special Education. Special Education comes through federal authority; therefore its programs are consistent from state to state (although names and acronyms for programs and processes do differ). Special Education has powerful implications within the school environment because it assures, by law, that the qualified student is afforded one-on-one special handling and instruction. The continuing need for, and the terms and conditions of, this special handling and instruction are the subject of a formal school meeting held annually. The purpose of this meeting is to develop the child's Individual Education Plan and, if necessary, a Behavior Management Plan.

Special Education services and placement are tied to what is called a Handicapping Condition, a reason *why* this youngster is eligible for special placement and programming. The Handicapping Condition for oppositional and defiant youngsters refers to psychological and emotional handicaps. Obviously this can only be determined *after* the youngster has been assessed by a psychiatrist or a psychologist, or someone acting under their authority. The formal *DSM-IV* diagnosis for this condition, Oppositional Defiant Disorder, has already been discussed in previous chapters.

Not a Panacea. Before you run out and get this special handling and instruction for your child, please read on. Although Special Education has been a godsend to many educators, parents, and students, it is *not* a perfect system. It will *not* solve all of your youngster's problems. In some cases, it might even contribute a few.

First of all, it is not automatic that your child will even qualify for these services. Many states and school districts have made a ruling that behavioral problems are not the same as emotional problems, and they will not consider a youngster with ODD for Special Education placement and programming because this diagnosis is chiefly behavioral. (One way around this problem is for the psychiatrist or psychologist to focus on features of *depression*, which will qualify, and which is usually present anyway.)

Even if the youngster goes through the assessment process and is determined to be eligible for Special Education placement and programming, he or she is going to be given a rather severe label—*Seriously Emotionally Disturbed* (a category name used in Texas), or something very similar to it. (On a lighter note, I was asked once to speak to a group of "EC" teachers in another state, and prepared a program for Early Childhood educators. I ended up speaking to teachers of the Emotionally Challenged. Big lesson: check it out!)

Even if you as a parent can live with the label of a diagnosis, can your child? Sometimes youngsters believe that now we think they're *crazy*! This helps neither their emotional state nor their subsequent behaviors. It is important that they be told how the system works, and how and why such a classification is used. I have found that a straightforward approach works the best.

Although Special Education placement and services bring assurance as to how the child will be served, there is no guarantee regarding effectiveness. It is possible that the youngster could be just as oppositional and defiant within a Special Education arrangement. If this is the case, then a whole lot of work and labeling has been for naught. Since teachers differ in their philosophy, methodology, and regard for young people, it is quite possible that a "regular" education teacher could be more effective with your youngster than a Special Education teacher. Programs don't provide quality education; teachers do.

If Your Child Is Placed. If the decision is made to place your child in Special Education, be very clear that placement and programming relate to the youngster's noncompliance. As a rule, oppositional and defiant youngsters do not have trouble understanding the schoolwork that they are asked to do; they have trouble getting it done. Since Special Education is often made available to youngsters who have learning disabilities (these students *do* have difficulty understanding schoolwork), it makes sense that teaching strategies and interventions for your child will be different from what is being provided for other students who might be in the same Special Education classroom.

With the clear understanding that the ability to do the work is not the issue (be clear on this, because oppositional and defiant children can also have learning disabilities), I always suggest a slightly different type of placement and programming. I usually recommend that the youngster be placed in a supportive resource-type class, which is preferably the last period of the school day. The primary focus of this class is for the child to finish all of that day's assignments at school, thus avoiding homework problems. I usually suggest that if the child finishes all of his or her work and turns it in before leaving school that day, the youngster can enjoy free time on the computer, be an office aide, or do something else that he or she would view as an incentive.

A Label-less Alternative. Just because a youngster is *eligible* for Special Education placement and services doesn't necessarily mean that providing them would be in his or her best interest. This is especially true whenever the primary concern is noncompliance—which it usually is.

If arrangements can be made for the youngster to finish work at school, such as before school begins, after school is out, or at other times during the school day, it is possible to address the main concerns while keeping this child within the regular classroom setting. A word of warning: I have found that such an arrangement usually works as well as, if not better than, actual Special Education placement; but it does require some real flexibility on the part of the school.

Accomplishing Compliance at School

Although I have no sleight-of-hand or slick magic to offer you as a solution, I feel very comfortable in affirming that the interventions covered here will work. They have already worked for the thousands of educators and counselors who have attended my school and university training programs on this youngster. You might want to show these to your child's teacher. Better yet, photocopy the order form at the end of this book, and encourage the school's librarian to add this book to the teachers' professional development section of the library. Every school should have one.

The process of encouraging this youngster to accomplish school-related tasks, which is far and away the most critical issue of compliance at school, can be divided into three simple and distinct parts: beginning the task, continuing the task, and completing the task.

These three are obviously connected. It would be pretty silly to expend an enormous amount of energy directing the child to begin the task, only to watch him fizzle out somewhere along the way.

Sometimes even the process of moving a student from beginning tasks to completing them is still not enough. When my son Jamie was in junior high school, he was the sixth-grade King of Noncompliance (he straightened out a bunch in high school, thanks to athletics). One teacher kept him after school to finish an assignment. He was required to show the completed assignment to the after-school tutorial teacher before he could go home.

Which was exactly what he did. After showing the paper to the teacher, who nodded approvingly, he casually tossed it onto a table in the library and left. The librarian found it the next day and put it in the teacher's box. Remember: a school task or assignment is never complete until it is recorded in the teacher's grade book.

The principles behind these interventions should be familiar to you by now; they follow the *Reduce* and *Raise* Formula (Chapter Thirteen). The accomplishment of school-related tasks is reached either by reducing elements of overdependency within the task (*Reduce*), or by raising the youngster's awareness of the noncompliant behaviors (*Raise*). In some cases, these strategies and interventions will simply be a spin-off of something used at home (as covered in Chapters Fourteen and Fifteen). They are summarized in Figure 16-2.

Task-Directed Interventions
- a summary -

Beginning the Task

1. Failproofing against misunderstanding
2. Failproofing against procrastination
3. Redirecting through paradox
4. Employing forced choice

Continuing the Task

1. Employing humor
2. Structuring progressively more difficult material
3. Using timers creatively

Finishing the Task

1. Using behavior modification
2. Writing contracts

Figure 16-2

Beginning the Task. These four strategies all relate to the important job of getting started on a task.

1. Failproofing against misunderstanding. This intervention deals effectively with the youngster who says, "I didn't understand what I was supposed to do," or who misinterprets and does a different task instead.

The fact that these misunderstandings are going to happen from time to time with students is not the issue. Rather, repetitive and persistent misunderstanding by the oppositional and defiant child is the target behavior for this intervention.

Armed with the understanding that this student does not really want to do damage to relationships with significant adults, the teacher simply asks for a favor. This child will almost always respond.

The teacher calls the child up to the desk, explains the assignment completely, then asks the child to write the assignment on the board so that all of the students can see it. The youngster is then asked to carefully explain the assignment to the entire class, and handle any questions that might come up. The teacher asks if everyone understands the assignment, and asks for a show of hands of those who do. Then the teacher asks the child to place his or her initials next to the assignment on the board. Finally, the youngster is thanked before returning to his or her seat.

It is very important that the assignment, complete with the youngster's initials, remain on the board until the assignment is due. If there is a concern that the board might accidentally be erased, have the youngster write the assignment on a piece of flip-chart paper, then tape the sheet to the wall. If there is concern that more than one youngster might "forget" or misunderstand the assignment, have *all* of the students walk up to the assignment sheet and initial it after it has been explained to them.

These students would have to be comatose to come back to the teacher later and say that they did not understand the assignment. Besides, it's still there on the board, complete with their autographs! Although this intervention will probably not effect a permanent cure with any child, it will help the teacher eliminate yet one more area of conflict. In this business, every little bit helps.

2. *Failproofing against procrastination.* If the teacher says, "This assignment is due on Friday," the oppositional and defiant child can have a field day. Exactly what does "This assignment is due on Friday" mean? Does it mean *this* Friday or *next* Friday? Does it mean that it is due when the school doors open at 7:30 a.m. on Friday morning, or is the assignment to be turned in during class? Can Johnny turn it in when his teacher is trying to eat her lunch in peace, or can he pass it to her through her car window at the end of the school day as she is heading out of the parking lot with little on her withered mind except two blissful days of weekend reprieve?

If it is due during class, does that mean when class starts, or when class is over? And when the teacher says Friday, does that really mean that he can stretch the agony out to the following Monday or Tuesday?

This youngster is a challenge; trying to pin him down on something as specific as a deadline can be like trying to nail Jell-O to a tree. Specifics are a must, even to the point that they appear ridiculous (keep in mind that humor is *also* an effective tool). The teacher might say:

> *"Class, this assignment is due Friday the 12th of this month. It is due anytime during class that day, and it will be counted late if it is not turned in when the dismissal bell rings. Assignments are to be placed in a green folder that will be right here on the upper left-hand corner of my desk. Assignments not placed in that folder will not be graded. Any assignments not graded will receive a zero in the grade book. Are there any questions? Raise your hand if you understand what the assignment is and when, where, and how it is due. Thank you. Johnny, please go to the board and write next to the assignment that everyone understands what the assignment is and when, where, and how it is due.* (Is there an echo in here?) *Please initial it also."*

3. Redirecting through paradox. The notion of "reverse psychology" refers to something that parents have been using on their children for years. It was discussed in Chapter Thirteen as a way to increase a youngster's awareness of his or her noncompliance, as well as awareness of what the noncompliance really means.

Whenever one of our children would wake up too sick to go to school, there was a simple test that my wife would use to tell how sick they were. With deepest empathy, she would say, "Oh, it looks like you'll have to stay home from school today. It's too bad, 'cause you'll miss Julie's birthday party this afternoon." Sometimes a miraculous healing would take place right before her eyes.

The term that psychologists and psychiatrists use for reverse psychology is "paradoxical intent," also called "paradoxical injunction." In application, they are all identical. As an intervention, paradoxical intent draws its power from the fact that it predicts, or permits, the child's oppositional and defiant behavior. As a result, it "steals their thunder"; the "reward" for noncompliance is removed.

Here's an example from the early elementary grades. It is time for recess, and the teacher is trying to take the class outside. One student, however, persistently tries to linger behind. With just a bit of pre-intervention planning for the safety and supervision of this child, the teacher can then do some redirection using paradox. She might say to the child:

> *"Joanie, I notice that every time we start to go to recess, you seem to prefer to stay in the room. Well, I think that is wonderful. We can use a room monitor to look after our things while we are out. So, when we go to recess tomorrow, I want you to stay back and be our room monitor. Okay?"*

If Joanie's behavior has been oppositional and defiant in intent, she will probably be the first one out the door when recess comes around again.

The intervention of paradoxical intent (or paradoxical injunction) can sometimes be used to encourage a youngster to attend to homework by simply announcing that he or she probably will not be able to do it:

> *"Listen, Johnny, this math worksheet is tough. I mean it's **really** tough. I looked through it, and I don't believe that I could answer more than two or three of the questions myself. I know that you will have trouble with it, but go ahead and give it your best shot. See how many you can do."*

Under such a challenge, the youngster might attack the work. Of course, he or she would probably be doing it to prove the teacher wrong. Although this is not the best of motives, it might create a spark of compliance.

Teachers are encouraged to use paradoxical intent with some degree of caution. First of all, it can quickly be overused. At that point it will become worthless as a task-directed intervention. Youngsters will quickly catch on to the fact that it is basically a deceptive ploy. Secondly, paradoxical intent can sometimes come across to the youngster as unkind and sarcastic. Sarcasm of any sort can do serious damage to relationships.

   4. Employing forced choice. Power is the one thing that young people clearly understand. They know when they have it, they know when they do not, and they know when they want it. The fact that oppositional and defiant children sense that their power is limited or blocked lies at the center of their problem behavior.

Power is realized when the child can influence changes in his or her environment. Change, good or bad, is the product of a decision. Decisions are possible only when there are choices. Ultimately, then, offering choices increases power.

As authentic power increases, oppositional and defiant behaviors usually decrease. They are no longer necessary.

The practice of offering the youngster choices can be highly effective (Chapter Fourteen). It is interesting to note that many folks find it to be rather profound as an intervention.

If the teacher wants Johnny to complete three tasks, for example, she can give him five assignments, with the instruction that he is to complete the three of his choice. If the order of their completion is not important, that's even better; he can choose that also.

If this intervention has a hidden secret that makes it work, it lies in the careful structuring of the five tasks. The teacher should be completely satisfied with any three tasks the youngster selects. Any argument from the teacher regarding the child's decision puts the whole thing back on the No-lutions roller coaster.

Continuing the Task. These three interventions focus on encouraging the youngster to continue working on the task.

1. Employing humor. As an intervention, humor is excellent because the oppositional and defiant youngster simply does not expect it. Whenever a student cannot predict the teacher's next response to his behavior, he forfeits control.

The use of humor is not only effective with this child, it is usually the easiest sort of intervention to put into motion. An example actually came my way while I was putting together this chapter. I was training a group of teachers in Graham, Texas, when one of them told me this interesting story:

> *"I put the whole class to working independently on an assignment, and was delighted to observe that Mark, my most oppositional and defiant student, was actually beginning the assignment without the usual hassles or delaying excuses—you know, needing a book from his locker, having no supplies, needing a drink, or wanting to go to the bathroom or to the pencil sharpener.*
>
> *For whatever reason, he was working away at his desk, writing profusely. Writing! I gave in to the urge to circle the date on my desk calendar.*
>
> *While assisting another student, I glanced at his paper. There was nothing on it—nothing! He was writing away alright, but his pen was poised just barely above the paper.*
>
> *I wanted to throttle him, Dr. Sutton. What should I have done?"*

At this point in the training that day, we had already discussed the No-lutions and how, whenever the teacher becomes upset at a student's behavior, that same behavior is guaranteed to occur again in the next similar set of circumstances. We talked about how, even though a teacher in this situation can intellectually and professionally *understand* the dynamics of what is going on, it is indeed quite difficult for that teacher to react differently when he or she is upset.

I remember telling this teacher that I would have used humor as an intervention. I added that I wouldn't think too much about it beforehand, for spontaneity would work in my favor; it generally does. Effective humor addresses a child's angry will without injuring a fragile and delicate spirit. Using humor (a form of overstatement in this case), a teacher could approach our furiously air-scribbling non-writer with something like this:

> *"(Gasp!) Whoa there, Mark! I think your pen just died! Yeah, that cotton-picker is dead alright. Let me see if I can find you one that will work before you forget all of that good stuff you're putting down."*

The teacher would then ask if someone might loan Mark a pen, then pause a moment to see if Mark can make the replacement work. Since this approach then brings his behavior to a deliberate level, the new pen should work just fine.

In this approach, confrontation of the youngster's intent can be avoided; so can the hassles.

If a teacher were to directly address the *intent* of Mark's oppositional or defiant behavior, the boy might see it as an open gesture to embarrass him. Asking him, for instance, to trade pens with another child would address his behavior alright ("See, there was nothing wrong with your pen. Quit causing so much trouble and get busy!"), but it would add to the youngster's resentment toward authority. It would also subtly encourage the child to come up with *another* oppositional and defiant way to get even.

The practice of skillfully bringing this child's behavior to a deliberate level will be more productive than confronting the intention of his behavior. Such a practice also allows for the improvement of relationships.

Understatement is another form of humor. When using understatement with a youngster, however, one must again be especially careful to avoid sarcasm.

When I was with the residential treatment center in San Antonio, one of the older adolescent girls from the facility was taken to school by her boyfriend. When he dropped her off that afternoon at the administration building, it looked as if they were having a free-for-all in the car. She stepped out of the vehicle and slammed the door so hard that her purse and books went flying. She gathered up her things, and came storming into the building.

"Hey Tanya," I called. She turned and glared at me with a look of pure poison. "I just wanted to say that it looks like you and John are not exactly ready to go down and pick out the furniture."

I paused, prepared to dodge anything that she might decide to throw at me.

She didn't say anything, but she did smile a little. More importantly, some of her anger seemed to vent.

Understatement, especially when it fits the situation naturally and spontaneously, can be a very useful and effective intervention.

    2. Structuring progressively more difficult material. Even when these youngsters begin work on an assignment, there is absolutely no assurance that they will continue with it. One of their handy excuses is an especially familiar one to teachers: "I can't do this, it's too hard!" with a look of pure misery accompanying the complaint.

The teacher or parent who is prepared for this tactic need not become upset or diverted from their own tasks.

"Well, Johnny, if that one's too hard for you, go get a worksheet out of that first box over there," the teacher might reply.

"Okay," he mumbles, as he reaches for the other assignment. He quickly recognizes, however, that there is a problem.

"Miss," he complains, "this one is harder than the first one!"

"Oh, then you might want to take a worksheet from that second box."

"Yeah, alright." As he reaches for the third worksheet, however, he realizes that it is much more difficult than either of the first two.

At this point, a light should come on—as he decides to stop playing this game and take the *first* worksheet. If he doesn't, the teacher can usually move the process along with, "Johnny, pick the one you want, but please get started."

After teachers use this intervention a few times with this youngster, they could eventually put their grocery list in the boxes. It simply will not matter, because these particular complaints should disappear.

3. Using timers creatively. My introduction to the creative use of timers came when I was working with Special Education programs in the schools. I was picking up some information from a teacher when she turned to redirect a youngster.

"Greg, if you don't get busy on that worksheet, I'm going to put you on the timer!"

The lad paled. "No, Miss! Please don't. Not the timer. Please, please, not the timer!"

"Then get busy." He got busy.

I was impressed. "What is it about the timer, Jan?" I asked.

"I haven't got a clue," she replied, "but it works."

Indeed it does. I believe that the success of this approach has to do with the competitive nature of the task and the fact that kids don't want to lose—not even to a timer.

A timer is an especially useful intervention for redirecting a child who is off task. A youngster is considered off task, for instance, whenever he is sent out to feed the dog, and ends up instead chasing a lizard into the next county. His *intention* might be one of compliance, but the compliance never happens.

In the classroom, this might be the child who camps out at the pencil sharpener. He spends so much time "getting ready" that he rarely does anything else. Though he seems to be so agreeable in spirit, the bottom line is that "getting ready" becomes his classroom career. From personal experience, I can assure you that this youngster is quite skilled at irritating the teacher.

Here's a strategy. The very next time that Johnny is off task, grinding the life out of another perfectly good pencil, the teacher could make the following announcement. It is directed to all the *other* youngsters who are at their desks and are on task.

> *"Class, it has been a long afternoon. Let me tell you what we are going to do. For those of you who are in your seats and working, I'm going to give you a five-minute sugarless candy break. And I'll even furnish the candy."*

The teacher then turns to address Johnny. By this time he knows full well that he has been set up.

> *"Johnny, I'll bet you're thinking that I waited until you were out of your seat to do this, aren't you?"*

"Darned right," the kid's thinking, but it doesn't much matter what he says. The smoke rolling out of his ears should tell the story.

"Listen, Johnny," the teacher comforts, "I'm going to do it again tomorrow, I promise." He'll stay in his seat. But even if Johnny briefly left his desk, I might wait until *after* he was back in his seat to be sure to cut him in on the candy deal. Reason: he would know that I was trying to be fair, which couldn't hurt the chances of his behavior improving.

This intervention warrants a closer look, because there is a built-in problem. Since this teacher decided when and where she was going to reward the on-task students, what about the notion of overdependency? That's right—it has been made worse, not better. If the intervention stopped at this point, the teacher might have the satisfaction of embarrassing the child, but no long-term benefit would come of it.

This is where the timer comes in handy again. A small timer can be set and hidden under a box, programmed to go off at random times during class. Youngsters who are on task when the timer sounds can receive a benefit or reward. One reward might consist of being able to write "free" next to a problem on the worksheet. In this case, compliance shortens the assignment and improves the grade. With this approach, it is the timer that calls the shots, not the teacher.

Finishing the Task. These two interventions consider ways of encouraging the youngster to finish and turn in tasks.

1. Using behavior modification (Grandma's Rule). Back in the '60s and '70s the absolute rave in education, especially Special Education, was something called "behavior modification." It was billed as a panacea, the magical solution to all learning challenges.

I remember sitting through class after class of this stuff, learning about things like baseline measures, schedules of reinforcement, extinction (of the behavior, not the child), and spontaneous recovery. As a class project, I used the principles on my little dog. I taught him to run to me immediately whenever I blew a whistle. After that little piece of research, the poor pooch would go nuts every time he heard a whistle of any kind. Although the study of the techniques of this intervention was exciting, and even though it certainly had its practical side, my subsequent experience in the classroom, and later as a practicing psychologist, brought me to two clear conclusions about the whole notion of behavior modification.

First of all, it was considerably oversold. Behavior modification is not magic. At its height of popularity, experts in this particular science exclaimed, "With behavior modification principles, it is possible to make someone into the President of the United States." There are folks who would say that we perhaps slipped a few into the White House just that way.

Although behavior modification as a formal intervention is being used in our schools today, it is primarily used with seriously handicapped youngsters, especially the mentally retarded, autistic, and seriously emotionally disturbed. There is no doubting its effectiveness with these populations.

The second conclusion notes the similarity between behavior modification and Grandma's Rule of "You'd better eat all of your peas if you want any apple pie." It might not be all that sophisticated, but heck—it works!

Grandma's Rule resides somewhere in the gene pool. Every parent knows how to use it on the kids. With a few creative twists, it can be used effectively with the oppositional and defiant student.

Obviously, doling out slices of apple pie in the classroom for work completed would not be all that practical (but a whole lot of fun!). Two things can be substituted for pastry. One would be any other sort of tangible rewards that appeal to the child. These goodies might include gum, coupons, money, stars, candy, and stickers. (When she was in the second grade, my daughter would have sold her own brother for a Scratch-N-Sniff sticker.)

The other kind of reward is one that involves an opportunity for the child to *do* something. A teacher utilizing such a reward for task completion might teach the child a neat magic trick, or let the child check out a new program on the computer, or send the child on a special errand to the office. These rewards are attractive to teachers because they are inexpensive and fairly easy to implement. And they contain no sugar.

Tangible rewards are not recommended for school-age oppositional and defiant youngsters, as they will likely opt for something even better. If the teacher offers them a sticker for completing the spelling assignment, they might go for what they can get by *not* completing the work. By simply doing nothing, this student can sit back and watch the teacher become frustrated, upset, red in the face, and angry, all at the same time. A front-row seat to this floor show beats a sticker any old day!

If a person studies what is going on here, it becomes obvious that a tangible reward is being offered for compliance, but an intangible and more powerful reward is being offered for noncompliance. The unfortunate part is that teachers are usually not aware of it. If they were aware, much oppositional and defiant behavior could be eliminated by simply planning more effective rewards.

A father came to my office a few years back. He was on the verge of tears. As a minister, he very much wanted his twelve-year-old oppositional and defiant son to participate in a Bible memory verses competition that his church was sponsoring.

The lad was not interested. To sweeten the pot, the father offered the boy $100 if he would compete. He even placed two $50 stacks of one-dollar bills in front of his son, pleading with him to participate. The boy refused; Dad was devastated.

In this case, behavior modification was being used, alright; it was being used on the *father*. Everything was running in the exact *wrong* direction. Dad would have had much more success had he approached his son with an intangible, activity sort of reward. With the oppositional and defiant student, intangibles work best in the classroom also.

Another approach that works surprisingly well with oppositional and defiant youngsters involves an item that I call the Magic Box (discussed near the end of Chapter Fifteen). It combines tangible and intangible rewards. The Magic Box is a wooden box about the size of a small backpack. It has a hinged lid with three to five hasps and locks on it. Before the contents inside the box can be obtained, a youngster must work his way through all of the locks.

The child is told that the instructions to a really impressive magic trick, or two quarters for the Coke machine, are in the box, and that he can have them whenever he can open it. As he completes assigned work, he is given a key to a lock. Opening the locks becomes a pleasant activity in itself, and each lock opened serves as an incentive to the end goal of enjoying the contents.

2. *Writing contracts.* Any effort directed at empowering the oppositional and defiant youngster will be productive. This is exactly why the previously mentioned intervention of forced choice works so well. A logical extension of this intervention is a negotiated contract with the child. The teacher sits down with the student and works out what tasks will be done, and when, where, and how they are to be completed and turned in. This intervention will work only if the child feels genuinely empowered to make selections from the choices available. When the youngster is part of the actual writing of the conditions of the contract, he or she is more apt to fulfill it.

The Homework Hassle

In the hands of an oppositional and defiant student, homework can be a deadly weapon. He can use it to exercise control and create serious problems.

The problem aspect stems from this child's built-in mechanism for "forgetting," a ploy that can be used to maximum benefit with homework. Another component to the problem is the fact that he can create, and knows that he can create, tremendous frustration with his parents and his teachers over this one highly flammable and irritating issue.

Although this youngster is not completing or turning in his schoolwork, rarely does he have any real difficulty *understanding* what he is to do. Even so, "Miss, I don't understand this" becomes one of his excuses of choice, along with his trusty standby of "I forgot."

Because this child can be a master of excuses, it is imperative that parents and teachers find a way to reach some sort of a united understanding regarding homework. They must see their respective roles clearly. If they do not, problems can occur whenever teachers and parents employ futile methods for helping this child remember his assignments. One such method (discussed in Chapter Fourteen) was the homework checklist. This intervention has too many holes—gaping spots where the youngster can create sabotage. What usually ends up getting lost and "forgotten" is the *checklist*.

Since the child's responsibility to the teacher is really the aim of homework in the first place, it is recommended that, whenever possible, the parents be spared this conflict. Frankly, they're going to have their hands full working to improve their own relationship with the youngster.

If homework is required, it is suggested that a structured time and place be provided for the youngster to complete it at school. Options could include before school, after school, during detention or tutorials, or even during a supportive resource (Special Education) arrangement. Such an approach better ensures that the work will be completed, and it prevents the assignments from being "lost" between home and school. Although this notion is difficult for some of the more traditionally oriented educators and parents to grasp sometimes, not sending work home will certainly cut off much of the fuel to the fire.

One teacher with a Gifted and Talented program shared with me that many of her students had trouble with the issue of homework. She decided to adjust her system to shut down homework as a source of friction.

This teacher requires no homework at all for a maximum grade of "B," and allows students to contract for an "A" by agreeing to do a certain amount of the work at home on their own. She shared that this arrangement continues to work splendidly, and that it has spared her some major grief.

"Go to the Office!" (Discipline)

Oppositional and defiant youngsters are not at risk for serious disciplinary action. They don't hurt people. They are more often in trouble for what they are *not* doing rather than what they *are* doing. Whenever occasion does find them in the office, they employ their social skills of politeness, deep "remorse," and an expressed desire to "get my act together." It's difficult to come down hard on a student who can seem so pitiful and so sincere.

Obviously, the occasions that find these youngsters in the school office will just about always involve two things: the student's noncompliance and the teacher's frustration. If the principal follows with yet another pleading or threatening lecture, the youngster may consider it a red-letter day of provoking adults.

If, however, the principal (or assistant principal), in understanding the dynamics unfolding here, decides to handle the youngster in a way that will address the nature of the child's refusal to do schoolwork, it is possible to effect a "cure." Such a "cure" requires a very carefully planned strategy. This strategy involves the commitment of the parents and the school to hold the child after school until he or she completes the work—whatever it takes.

Using this intervention, the parents, teacher, and principal agree upon a day when the youngster can be kept after school to finish an assignment. The parents are told that whenever the youngster finally makes it home, they are not even to mention the assignment or the lateness of the hour.

An elementary school principal shared with me the specifics of how this intervention was accomplished with a certain fifth grader at his school:

> *"I told Jimmy that he could finish the worksheet in a room adjacent to my office. I carefully explained that it was important that he not rush through it.* (Note the paradoxical intent.) *I told him that I needed access to the computer to work on my doctoral dissertation, so I would be working in the office until very late that evening. I again stressed to him that he need not hurry or rush, and that I would drive him home whenever he was finished.*
>
> *As I expected, he had a ball for the first hour or so. He waved at his friends as they*

were leaving the school, and he made several trips to the bathroom, the pencil sharpener, and the water fountain.

During the second hour, however, he became a bit more concerned. He seemed a bit rattled. He asked if he could just do it at home and bring it back the next day. I again told him that I was going to be at the school for some time, and that it was fine for him to go ahead and finish it there near my office.

At one point he even said that he felt sick, so I allowed him to stretch out on the little couch in the nurse's station until he felt well enough to continue on the worksheet. I was surprised that he did actually go to the nurse's station, but it was no time at all before he came back.

During the third hour I sent out for a pizza. Walking into his little room with a steaming slice of the pizza in my hand, I asked him how it was going, and again I encouraged him not to rush. I made certain to waft the aroma in his direction, then I left. Less than ten minutes later Jimmy showed up in my doorway with the completed worksheet.

I glanced over it to make certain that he had done acceptable work, then I put it in his teacher's box, grabbed my keys, and took him home.

> *While driving him home in the car, I made certain not to launch into a lecture about responsibility and how he could have saved himself a few hours of his own time. The whole thing worked like a charm; we have never had to repeat the intervention."*

It took a considerable amount of work and planning to set up this intervention, but it certainly seemed worth the effort. Everyone involved was able to benefit from it.

A principal in Nebraska told me of an interesting twist on this intervention. He offers to stay after school with youngsters while they complete their work, but he tells them that any teacher, counselor, or principal who stays after school in this fashion must be paid $10 an hour. He then offers to line the youngsters up with a job so they can pay for the tutoring (he will not let the parents pay it). Youngsters learn pretty quickly that they can save a lot of time and effort by just completing their schoolwork.

Chapter Seventeen

Growth Moves Toward the Future

There Comes a Time

Nowhere in this book have I promised a miracle. I will promise you this much. If even a few of the strategies and interventions included in this book are earnestly employed, they *will* have a positive impact on a youngster's behaviors. Such an impact can be either temporary or lasting depending upon the depth of your understanding about what is going on, how that understanding is turned into intervention, and, of course, the nature of the child or adolescent.

If everything goes well, there will come a time when the child's contribution to the relationship will no longer be fueled and maintained by fear, resentment, anger, spite, and revenge. It is a special time, a time that brings with it an almost magical quality—a quality of changing directions, with the knowledge that now things are headed in a much *better* direction.

Luke Revisited

In writing this book and making it available to folks, I am concerned that there might be those who are *only* interested in the interventions. They might try to shortcut the process of really trying to understand the youngster *behind* the oppositional and defiant behaviors. It is my opinion that, although they might enjoy some success with this child, what they would be doing amounts to manipulation and outright trickery. Above all else, the oppositional and defiant child hates to be tricked. This youngster can tolerate and even forgive mistakes that are made in moments of desperation, frustration, oversight, and yes, even anger. Harm that a parent inflicts *intentionally*, however, can do more damage to a child than I could ever begin to cover in this book.

Luke's parents back in Chapter Seven did the right thing by Luke, and they did it without the benefit of this book or any others. Sure, they had a little direction about what they should do, but most of it was intuitive. The bottom line was that they *loved* their son—and Luke knew it.

How did Luke know that his parents loved him? Time after time, they told him and they showed him. All of Luke's life they had demonstrated their integrity and their respect for each other and for their son. When they told Luke that they would not hold his honest response against him, he believed them. He simply believed them. I cannot overemphasize the value of integrity and respect when they are communicated within relationships.

Luke's parents also demonstrated patience. They seemed to understand that the hard feelings the boy had tucked away for years don't always surface quickly or even on command. These parents, especially Dad, expressed their vulnerability in a willingness to admit that they had made mistakes with Luke. In doing so, they modeled a truth that Luke will pass on to *his* children—that parents are people, and people make mistakes.

Even though the changes that they wanted their son to make were certainly a priority for Luke's folks, they were still willing to put *his* needs before their own. In doing so, they sent the message of "You are important to us." With all that much going for this little parent-child trio, why wouldn't there be some real improvement? Indeed.

If you'll just use Luke's folks as a model for what to do as a parent of an oppositional and defiant child, I don't see where you could go wrong.

Where Does It Go?

Back in Chapter Two, needs were discussed as they affected goal-setting and the stability of a person's behavior. Whenever there are problems concerning the needs of Security, Order, Belonging, Worth, Approval, Stimulation, and Growth, progress is impeded. The feelings of fear and anger are then released like a raging swarm of bees.

Question: Where does all the energy of these feelings go when relationships begin to mend? If for years that energy was being dumped into oppositional and defiant behavior, where does it go when it is no longer needed?

I have an answer to this question; it might surprise you. I don't believe that the energy goes anywhere in particular. I also believe that the youngster doesn't have a clue regarding what to do with it. But it is energy just the same, and it can be channeled into some wonderful and positive directions. The youngster must be shown and taught how to do this.

Your "Casual" Opinion

After years of working with oppositional and defiant youngsters and their families and teachers, I have come to realize two truths regarding improvement in behaviors and relationships. First of all, your children care about your opinions, impressions, and interpretations of their progress and improvement. They won't say much about it to you, and they might even act like they don't really care. But they do. After all, what would be the use of trying to change if no one noticed?

The second truth is that, especially initially, it is possible to talk too much about improvement—even to the point of aggravating the youngster out of trying any further.

A dilemma exists, then, of not saying enough to your child on the one hand, yet saying too much on the other. The best way to solve this problem is to speak about improvement *around* your child, but not necessarily *to* your child. Now, the first time you do this your son or daughter might think that you have taken to talking to the walls, but they *will* like what they hear.

There are a couple of ways you could mention improvements indirectly. You might, for instance, address your comments in general or to another person in the room (of course, the child is in the room also). Make an observation, then follow it up with an interpretation of some sort, such as, "I haven't had to make a case about homework around here all week; that kind of responsibility really impresses me," or "I just checked the list, and every single chore has been done for three days straight; it's really great when we don't have to hassle over the small stuff." You might want to add, "In fact, I think we should celebrate! I'm going for ice cream."

Another way to make constructive comments is similar to the SPCs (Strategically Placed Compliments) that were discussed in Chapter Fifteen. Make your comments directly to the child, but in an offhand "Oh, by the way" fashion. I'm convinced that what parents say casually to a child carries as much weight as what they say formally. Speaking to the youngster in a casual manner lets the child know that you did notice, but does not require a response from them. This is best done whenever you or your child is getting ready to leave the house or just about to change to another activity. An example:

> *"By the way, Susan, before you leave, I*
> *just wanted to let you know that I appreciate*
> *the effort you are putting into your*

> *homework, and I am very impressed with the improvements you have made."*

Hopefully, Susan will already be on her way out the door, and won't feel any pressure to respond. If this is not the case, try to have something that quickly needs your attention, to avoid getting into a discussion at this time regarding what you have said. That will be the job of the Victory List, to be described next.

The Victory List Challenge

Whenever I do therapy or counseling with a group of children or adolescents, I like to open the session by asking each person to tell the group their name, and then to answer this question:

> *What was the most significant thing that you accomplished during the past six months?*

It's a tough enough question for kids, but it drives adults absolutely nuts because, as a rule, we tend to focus too much on our shortcomings—*not* on our victories. And, unfortunately, there is also a tendency to impress this same behavior on our children.

As important as it is for you to let your son or daughter know that you recognize their progress, it is also important that *they* begin to recognize their progress, and keep it going. This is not always automatic, but you can help.

Encourage every member of the family to keep a Victory List for the week (Figure 17-1). On their list each person is to write down those things that represented accomplishments to them. Keep the list short to begin with, perhaps only three items. Too many items will overburden the child and cause him or her to dislike working with the list. This would quickly defeat the whole purpose of the activity (and probably even encourage oppositional and defiant behavior).

My Victory List

1. _____

   _____

2. _____

   _____

3. _____

   _____

Figure 17-1

On a regular basis the family should come together, and everyone should have an opportunity to share their three most significant victories for the week. What is interesting about this activity is that the parents will likely have been unaware of some of the victories of their children, and the children might not have thought to include some victories that the parents could point out. This makes for a great time of sharing, and it's all centered around accomplishments— *not* problems.

After the Victory List activity is going well, you can add an interesting twist to it. Let everyone fill out their own Victory List, then also a list on each other family member. When everyone comes together, they can share and compare the week's victories.

Gratitude in Action

Gratitude is an essential quality for long-term mental health and for the enjoyment of positive relationships. Without action, however, gratitude alone is empty. It must be shared.

It's far too easy to have gratitude without action. What a waste. Gratitude put into action is a type of reverse blaming (blaming and spitefulness were among the typical oppositional and defiant behaviors covered in Chapter Three). It's a pretty effective cure for resentment and bitterness.

Alex Haley, the author of *Roots*, was said to have a certain picture in his office. It showed a turtle sitting on a fencepost. Haley would explain that the turtle did not get there by itself; it had some help. What a message. All of us need a little help from others from time to time, and we need to express our gratitude for that help.

Since it takes the best part of a person to recognize the best part of another person, it is important that the oppositional and defiant youngster learn, in time, how to express his or her appreciation in a genuine and powerful fashion. Everyone involved will benefit.

Try a weekly Gratitude List, then encourage the youngster and other family members to brainstorm some very specific ways to express that gratitude to the individuals involved. Encourage creativity.

As a parent, it would be helpful if you model this for your children. It is important that you actually *do* send the flowers or the card, or make the phone call. Although it's easier *not* to do it, it's not all that hard to be expressive with thanks.

Goal-Setting

As the youngster begins to stabilize in his or her needs (meaning that there is not as much anger and fearfulness as before), it is time to direct old energy into positive avenues of goal-setting.

Although goal-setting should be taught to all youngsters whether they're oppositional and defiant or not, it is surprising to see how little time public schools spend on teaching this skill. Goal-setting is a excellent tool of empowerment and direction.

The process for goal-setting is not difficult, but it is important not to start it until the youngster is able to express some interest in it. Figure 17-2 shows a Goals Worksheet. It lists nine specific categories that could be the focus of goal-setting, plus an "other." Not all youngsters will be interested in tackling all ten of them, and not all of them are appropriate for younger children, but the list is adaptable.

Encourage the youngster to come up with a couple of goals for each category selected. Offer support and direction, but let the child work out the specifics of the goals. Next, ask the youngster to write down some sort of time frame for the expected completion of each goal. This might be expressed in weeks, months, or years, but it is best for the youngster to have some long-term and some short-term goals (achievement of short-term goals will encourage the child to continue to use the process). Then instruct the child to put an "A," "B," or "C" rating beside each goal. The "A" represents the goals that the child most desires to accomplish. This will hopefully serve to weed out those goals that were not really the child's own.

The youngster is then encouraged to look at the "A" goals (the most desired), and determine what it will take in terms of resources to achieve them. The youngster will learn that resources can include a number of things: money, transportation, assistance from others, and so on. At this point the child is ready to determine what can be done today, this week, this month, and this year to effectively reach the goal. This includes planning and calling upon the resources.

The last step, of course, is the actual work toward the goals themselves. Encourage the youngster to keep careful written records of steps taken to achieve the goals, and of the progress noted.

● Goals Worksheet

Personal Habits/Characteristics:

Health/Physical:

Career:

Financial/Property:

● Educational/Learning:

Recreation:

Home/Family:

Social:

Spiritual:

● Other:

Figure 17-2

Make it a point to celebrate goals when they are achieved. Don't forget to have a party! It is a critical part of goal-setting.

(An excellent reference on goal-setting is a six-cassette program by Zig Ziglar entitled *The Goals Program*. The effectiveness and credibility of this program is underscored by Zig's own life. He practices what he preaches. *The Goals Program* is available through the Zig Ziglar Corporation by calling 800-527-0306.)

From Understanding to Outstanding

Insight is something that can come to us out of the blue. We can be going along, doing what we have always done, and then *wham!*—it hits us that there is another, better, and more productive way. It is not unusual for me to read evaluations from attendees of my all-day program on the oppositional and defiant youngster and come across one like this:

> *I realized today that I was one of these kids. It has caused me and my loved ones too much grief for much too long. Starting today, I intend to make some changes.*

The gratifying conclusion to this realization is that when I go back with another program a year or so later, that person tells me *how* they have changed.

I mention this in closing this chapter and this book to encourage you to be there to help light the spark of insight in your child. Insight is not something you plan; you can only make yourself available to allow it to happen. It might come quickly or it might take years, but it *will* make an appearance.

When your child gets to the point of recognizing and interpreting compliance, when he or she begins to invest more completely in relationships with others and shows initiative toward growth, then you've done your job.

Congratulations!

If My Kid's So Nice ... Why's He Driving ME Crazy?

Glossary

ADD Attention-Deficit Disorder. See "ADHD."

ADHD Attention-Deficit/Hyperactivity Disorder, a neurological condition of children which is developmental in nature. Its primary symptoms include impulsivity, hyperactivity, and difficulty with attention and concentration. ADD (Attention-Deficit Disorder) is the same condition, but without hyperactivity.

Affect The physical representation of an emotional state, including voice, facial expression, mannerisms, and posturing.

Anxiety A state of internal agitation, usually associated with fear and apprehension. Most anxiety is specific to the condition or circumstances causing it. Sometimes, however, anxiety is generalized. Generalized anxiety is more difficult to treat.

Behavior Modification The carefully structured use of rewards (reinforcement) to bring about desired behavior.

Behavioral Continuum See "Continuum of Behavior."

Childhood Psychiatric Disorders That section of the *DSM-IV* that describes psychiatric conditions of children and adolescents.

Comorbidity   The circumstance of two or more conditions or disorders being diagnosed simultaneously in the same individual (such as ADHD and ODD).

Compliance   The completion of behaviors and tasks at the request of an adult authority figure.

Conduct Disorder   A very serious *DSM-IV* disorder of children and adolescents that is manifested by the breaking of major age-appropriate societal rules and norms. Aggression and law-breaking behavior are often associated with Conduct Disorder.

Congenital   A descriptive term explaining a condition that is present at birth.

Congruency   A "match" between affect and mood. For example, a person who is experiencing depression, and *appears* to be depressed, would be demonstrating congruency.

Continuum of Behavior   The author's term for behaviors of children and adolescents as they exist on a line from left (very appropriate) to right (very inappropriate).

Denial   An ego defense mechanism manifested by the conscious rejection of the notion that an issue exists.

Depression   A suppression of mood (and usually affect also), which is experienced as sadness.

DSM   The *Diagnostic and Statistical Manual of Mental Disorders*, as published by the American Psychiatric Association. There have been five editions. The most recent, the *DSM-IV*, was published in 1994.

Dynamic Issue A psychologically "deep" issue, from which other issues arise.

Evaluation The assessment of an individual in order to determine the presence of a condition, disorder, or disability.

Expectations Standards for behavior and achievement that a parent communicates to a child. These can be expressed to the child, or they can be strongly implied without actual expression. Expectations can be general ("I expect you to be honest and truthful") or quite specific ("I expect you to go to law school after you graduate high school, then join your grandfather and me in the firm").

"Good Kid" Disorder The author's descriptive term for Oppositional Defiant Disorder as it applies to youngsters who have and understand social and family "connections." The term also applies to those youngsters who have never been formally diagnosed as ODD, but who display some of the symptoms and behaviors. Youngsters with the "Good Kid" Disorder rarely engage in aggressive, violent, or law-breaking behavior.

Grandma's Rule A predecessor of Behavior Modification. Grandma would apply the Rule by saying to a child, "You can have some pie *after* you eat all of your peas."

Handicapping Condition A disorder or disability that qualifies a youngster for Special Education placement and programming.

Hyperactivity Excess of physical energy in a child that often makes it difficult for the youngster to comply. Hyperactivity is one symptom of ADHD.

Hyperkinesis Basically another term for hyperactivity. Hyperkinesis is generally used as a medical term.

Incongruency The lack of a "match" between affect and mood. For example, an individual appears to be happy and serene when, in fact, his or her emotional state is in turmoil.

Intervention A strategy or collection of strategies aimed at reducing oppositional and defiant behavior and the issues that create it.

Issue A specific concern or problem within a relationship. A child who never completes homework would have an issue with a teacher.

Minimization An ego defense mechanism manifested by marginal recognition of an issue, with an attempt to make light of it.

Mood The emotional state of an individual at any one point in time.

No-lutions The author's term for a collection of seven ways that adults typically address oppositional and defiant behavior in children. They are intended to be solutions, but they rarely bring about long-term improvement in behavior.

Noncompliance The refusal of a child or adolescent to complete behaviors or tasks as requested by an adult authority figure.

ODD See "Oppositional Defiant Disorder."

Oppositional and Defiant Behavior Any of the behaviors associated with Oppositional Defiant Disorder. It is possible for a child to exhibit some of these behaviors and never formally be diagnosed as ODD.

Oppositional Defiant Disorder A childhood psychiatric condition, as included in the *DSM-IV*. Annoying behaviors of oppositionality and defiance toward authority figures typify this disorder.

Oppositional Disorder An earlier *DSM* term for Oppositional Defiant Disorder.

Overdependency A term borrowed from an early edition of the *DSM*. For a child or adolescent, it refers to the loss of a sense of autonomy, direction, or independence due to restrictions imposed by an adult authority figure.

Paradoxical Injunction See "Paradoxical Intent."

Paradoxical Intent A strategy or intervention for preventing a behavior by suggesting to a youngster that he or she is probably going to engage in that behavior.

Passive Aggression An older term for oppositional and defiant behavior. It can be a feature of ODD. Specifically, passive aggression is the indirect or unassertive expression of aggression toward others.

Passive-Aggressive An adjective that expresses the characteristics of Passive Aggression.

Progression of Deviancy The author's term for a chart depicting behavioral conditions and disorders along a continuum of behavior. See "Continuum of Behavior."

Psychiatrist   A physician who specializes in the diagnosis and treatment of mental disorders and conditions.

Psycho-Behavioral Bind   The author's term for the circumstance that occurs when an individual has an issue with an authority figure, but cannot confront that figure directly for fear of catastrophic consequences.

Psychologist   A doctorate-level mental health professional (not a physician) who, among other things, performs assessments, conducts therapy, and develops and implements programs of behavioral management.

Repression   An ego defense mechanism whereby awareness of an issue is subconsciously suppressed. An individual does not control repression.

Reverse Blaming   The author's term for describing the quality of expressing gratitude.

Reverse Psychology   See "Paradoxical Intent."

Special Education   Individualized educational programming for youngsters identified as having a Handicapping Condition.

Strategically Placed Compliment   The author's term for a special type of compliment that a youngster will not reject. With this technique, the compliment is immediately followed by a question to the child. It is intended that the youngster will respond to the question, and not spoil or reject the compliment.

Treatment   A term for an intervention or group of interventions that are considered to be clinical or medical in purpose.

References

Algozzine, R., *Teaching the mildly handicapped*. A program presented at the Texas Conference on Emotional Disturbance, Austin, Texas: February, 1981.

American Psychiatric Association, *Diagnostic and statistical manual of mental disorders II*. Washington, D.C.: APA, 1968.

_____, *Diagnostic and statistical manual of mental disorders III*. Washington, D.C.: APA, 1980.

_____, *Diagnostic and statistical manual of mental disorders III-R*. Washington, D.C.: APA, 1987.

_____, *Diagnostic and statistical manual of mental disorders IV*. Washington, D.C.: APA, 1994.

Anderson, J., Williams, S., McGee, R., Silva, P., "DSM-III Disorders in preadolescent children." *Archives of General Psychiatry* 1987; 44:69-76.

Barkley, R., *Defiant children: a clinician's manual for parent training*. New York: Guilford Press, 1987.

Biederman, J., Newcorn, J., Sprich, S., "Comorbidity of attention deficit hyperactivity disorder with conduct, depressive, anxiety, and other disorders." *American Journal of Psychiatry* 1991; 148:564-577.

Cantwell, D., Baker, L., "Stability and natural history of DSM-III childhood diagnoses." *Journal of the American Academy of Child and Adolescent Psychiatry* 1989; 28:691-700.

Cohen, P., Velez, N., Kohn, M., Schwab-Stone, M., Johnson, J., "Child psychiatric diagnosis by computer algorithm." *Journal of the American Academy of Child and Adolescent Psychiatry* 1987; 26: 631-638.

Gard, G., Berry, K., "Oppositional children: taming tyrants." *Journal of Clinical Child Psychology* 1986; 15:148-158.

Hancock, L., "Mother's little helper." *Newsweek*; March 18, 1996; 51-55.

Kashani, J., Beck, N., Hoeper, E., Reid, J., "Psychiatric disorders in a community sample of adolescents." *American Journal of Psychiatry* 1987; 144:584-589; correction 144:1114.

Lahey, B., Loeber, R., Quay, H., Frick, P., Grimm, J., "Oppositional defiant and conduct disorders: issues to be resolved for DSM-IV." *Journal of the American Academy of Child and Adolescent Psychiatry* 1992; 31(3):539-545.

Levy, D., "Oppositional syndromes and oppositional behavior," in *Psychopathology of Childhood.* Edited by Hoch, P., Zubin, J. New York: Grune and Stratton, 1955.

Long, N., *Teaching the emotionally disturbed child.* A workshop presented for Region XX Education Service Center consumers, San Antonio, Texas: November, 1976.

McGee, R., Freehan, M., Williams, S., Partridge, F., Silva, P., Kelly, J., "DSM-III disorders in a large sample of adolescents." *Journal of the American Academy of Child and Adolescent Psychiatry* 1990; 29:611-619.

McMahon, R., Forehand, R., "Parent training for the noncompliant child: treatment outcome, generalization, and adjunctive therapy procedures," in *Parent training: foundations of research and practice.* Edited by Dangel, R., Polster, R. New York: Guilford Press, 1984; 298-328.

Meeks, J., "Behavioral and antisocial disorders," in *Basic Handbook of Child Psychiatry*, vol 2. Edited by Noshpitz, J. New York: Basic Books, 1979.

Morrison, E., "Underachievement among preadolescent boys considered in relation to passive aggression." *Journal of Educational Psychology* 1969; 60(3):168-173.

Peck, M., *A world waiting to be born: rediscovering civility*. New York: Bantam Books, 1993; 283.

Pelham, W., "Teacher ratings of DSM III-R symptoms for the disruptive disorders." *Journal of the American Academy of Child and Adolescent Psychiatry* 1992; 31:210-218.

Rey, J., "Oppositional defiant disorder." *American Journal of Psychiatry* 1993; 150(12):1769-1778.

Rey, J., Bashir, M., Schwarz, M., Richards, I., Plapp, J., Stewart, G., "Oppositional disorder: fact or fiction?" *Journal of the American Academy of Child and Adolescent Psychiatry* 1988; 27:157-162.

Rutter, M., Shaffer, D., "DSM-III: a step forward or back in terms of the classification of child psychiatric disorders." *Journal of the American Academy of Child Psychiatry* 1980; 19:371-394.

Spitzer, R., Davies, M., Barkley, R., "The DSM III-R field trials of disruptive behavior disorders." *Journal of the American Academy of Child and Adolescent Psychiatry* 1990; 29:690-697.

Sutton, J., *Passive aggressive features of oppositional disorder: effects of specific training on teacher attitudes toward these behaviors in students.* Doctoral dissertation: Brigham Young University, 1981.

_____, *Children of crisis, violence, and loss.* Pleasanton, Texas: Friendly Oaks Publications, 1995.

_____, *The oppositional and defiant child.* A workshop for child service professionals: Pleasanton, Texas, 1995.

Wenning, K., Nathan, P., King, S., "Mood disorders in children with oppositional defiant disorder: a pilot study." *American Journal of Orthopsychiatry* 1993; 63(2):295-299.

Werry, J., "Attention deficit, conduct, oppositional, and anxiety disorders in children: a review of research in differentiating characteristics." *Journal of the American Academy of Child and Adolescent Psychiatry* 1987; 26:133-143.

Index

We have included this order form for those who would like to make *If My Kid's So Nice ... Why's He Driving ME Crazy?* available to friends, relatives, clients, teachers and counselors.

Order Form

Price: $18.95

Sales tax: Add 8.25% if order is from Texas

Shipping/Handling: Add $4.50

Payment Method: (check one)

____Check/money order   ____Visa   ____MasterCard

Card number: _____

Expiration date: _____

Name on card: _____

Send orders to:

Friendly Oaks Publications
PO Box 662
Pleasanton, TX 78064

Phone orders: Call (830) 569-3586 or fax to (830) 281-2617

Ship books to:

Name: _____

Address: _____

City/State/Zip: _____

Dr. Sutton is an accomplished platform presenter; he holds the highest earned designation in professional speaking—*Certified Speaking Professional*. He is available for keynote presentations, conferences and workshops. He can be contacted through the following address:

Dr. James D. Sutton
% *Friendly Oaks Publications*
PO Box 662
Pleasanton, TX 78064-0662
(830) 569-3586

Since its start-up in 1990, *Friendly Oaks Publications* has been producing resources for parents and child service professionals. In 13 years of operation, *Friendly Oaks Publications* has published a total of 65 titles, including written works and recorded materials—the efforts of 20 authors.

Printed in the United States
17739LVS00003B/1-60

9 781878 878656